D1166567

344 QUESTIONS: THE CREATIVE PERSON'S DO-IT-YOURSELF GUIDE TO INSIGHT, SURVIVAL, AND ARTISTIC FULFILLMENT

STEFAN G. BUCHER

New Riders
1249 Eighth Street
Berkeley, CA 94710
510/524-2178
510/524-2221 (fax)

Find us on the Web at:
www.newriders.com
To report errors, please
send a note to
errata@peachpit.com

New Riders is an imprint of Peachpit,
a division of Pearson Education.

Acquisitions Editor
Production Editor
Design

Nikki Echler McDonald
Tracey Croom
Stefan G. Bucher for 344design.com
Timothy Moraitis for moraitisdesign.com

ISBN 13 978-0-321-73300-9
ISBN 10 0-321-73300-2

9 8 7 6 5 4 3 2

Printed and bound in China (CTPS/02)

344 QUESTIONS?

THE CREATIVE PERSON'S
DO-IT-YOURSELF GUIDE
TO INSIGHT, SURVIVAL,
AND ARTISTIC FULFILLMENT

WRITTEN & DESIGNED BY
STEFAN G. BUCHER

MY ANSWERS WON'T DO YOU ANY GOOD.

Sure, if you ask me something specific in person, I can probably be of some service to you. Sumi ink. Compressed air. Second door on the left, up the stairs, ask for Manny. And yes, you can borrow my pen. But beyond that? What can I tell you that isn't just a good guess at what might be helpful to you? The border between "universal" and "generic" is not always clearly defined. Being specific makes for better reading, but the particulars of my life aren't yours. And when it comes to life the particulars matter.

Let's be clear:

I WANT THIS BOOK TO BE USEFUL TO YOU.

There are many great how-to books and biographies out there, and even more gorgeous collections of current and classic work to awe and inspire. But looking at catalogs of artistic success won't make you a better artist any more than looking at photos of healthy people will cure your cold. You've got to take action!

Questions are very useful that way. I may have never met you, but I'm pretty sure, "What do you want to do next?" applies to you. Maybe, "What's keeping you from starting?" hits the mark, too? We are all different people, but we face a lot of the same questions.

The point of this book is to give you *lots* of questions you can use to look at your life—in a new way, with a different perspective, or maybe just in more detail than you have before—so you can find out how you work, what you want to do, and how you can get it done in a way that works for you. Specifically. This book has over 1,800 questions. Even if only 10% of them feel like they apply directly to your situation, that's 180 questions for you right there.

The more honest you are with yourself as you go through the book, and the more notes you make in it, the more valuable it will become to you. That's why this book is small, flexible, and doesn't cost a lot of money. I want you to take it with you when you go to work, keep it in your bag, and scribble into it as answers occur to you. Don't keep this book clean! Mess it up! Write in it freely! Doodle! Put a rubber band around it, so that you can keep interesting articles and extra pages of notes in it. If you keep this book in mint condition, I've failed. Because a tattered, busted-up book—filled out, and scribbled upon—means you've found out new things about yourself and you're inspired to take action.

In fact, will you do me a favor? Please dog-ear one of the pages right now, and write a swear word in the margin. Just to get started.

Of course, some of the questions are leading, and you'll probably have no trouble guessing how I'd answer some of them. But this isn't a hidden polemic. I really tried to keep the questions as open as possible. That's the whole point. What's worked well for me might be a disaster for you, and the things that make me crazy with anxiety might be worth no more than a bored yawn to you.

Your answers are what matter here.

And hey, even if you get tired of my questions after a while, there are over 500 questions by 38 amazing, thoughtful, funny, and always creative people in the book. Multiple points of view are helpful when it comes to looking at your own life, and sometimes it's just easier to hear these questions from people whose work you admire. (I don't know how you feel about the group I selected, but you better believe that I love the work they do.)

I designed the book as a sequence. There is a benefit to working through the whole thing from front to back. But you can just as easily jump to the sections that are the most pressing for you right now. You might consider putting a date on some of the pages, or even individual answers, so you can come back to them over time to see how your thoughts change as your circumstances do. Sometimes life evolves so gradually that you don't even notice what's really happening unless you create a record for yourself.

So there! Enough with the introduction!

Turn the page! Get to work!

See you on the other side!

ARE
NOW?

No, not literally. In a *larger* sense. Don't let the bright colors fool you. I'm being *serious*.

Not *that* serious, though.

Please feel free to doodle in the margins.

WOULDN'T THIS BE A GOOD PLACE TO START?

ARE YOU DOING WHAT YOU LOVE?

WHAT *ARE* YOU DOING?

IF YOU FIND THIS BOOK, PLEASE
☐ DISCARD IT ☐ RETURN IT TO:

Just write whatever comes to your mind.

Or draw it, if you like.

I'm asking about your life goals and such, but if you crave a sandwich, certainly jot that down, too.
It's your book, and you can use it any way you like.

WHAT DO YOU WANT?

Go ahead! I won't judge. Nor will the book.
It's printed on judgement-free paper.

DO YOU HAVE SECRET DESIRES YOU DON'T WANT ANYBODY TO KNOW ABOUT? WHY DON'T YOU WRITE THEM HERE, REALLY SMALL, AND THEN BLACK THEM OUT WITH A SHARPIE LATER ON?
(It'll still help to write this stuff down.)

OK. The really, really TOP SECRET DESIRE?
Wanna write that one here? If blacking it out isn't safe enough, you can just tear off this corner of the page and eat it when you're done.

NAME FIVE THINGS THAT YOU THINK
WILL HAPPEN FOR YOU THIS YEAR:

1.

2.

3.

4.

5.

WHAT ARE YOUR

IN BROAD STROKES, HOW DO YOU THINK

It's a big question, I know. But I bet you've thought about it before. And if you haven't, just let your mind wander for a while. Take a few minutes. Hell, take a few days. Sleep on it.

DO YOU THINK YOU'RE BORN TO GREATNESS?

WHAT MAKES YOU THINK THAT?

DO YOU LIKE YOUR EXPECTATIONS?

EXPECTATIONS?

DO YOU CONSIDER YOURSELF LUCKY?

CHARMED EVEN?

IN ANY PARTICULAR AREA OF LIFE?

WHY?

YOUR LIFE WILL UNFOLD?

DO YOU THINK YOU'RE AVERAGE?

DO YOU THINK YOU SUCK?

DO YOU HAVE ANY EVIDENCE?

Alright, this is all about questions, but if you really think that, let me just say right now that YOU DO NOT SUCK. I've been there, and I know that it can feel very real, but just trust me on that one, OK? OK. We'll talk more about this a few pages from now. For now, just bear with me. This book is on your side!

WHETHER YOU DO OR DON'T, HOW CAN YOU PUSH YOURSELF FURTHER?

WHO ARE YOUR HEROES?

WHAT DO YOU ADMIRE ABOUT THEM?

WHO ARE YOUR ENEMIES?

I do hope that your list of heroes is a lot longer than your list of enemies.

And that I won't end up on it. I mean well. I really do.

YES, NIXON HAD AN ENEMIES LIST, AND NOW YOU CAN, TOO.

These can be actual people, or you can take it down a more metaphorical path.

DO THEY KNOW THAT THEY'RE ON YOUR LIST?

DO THEY CARE?

DOES IT HELP YOU TO HAVE HEROES?

DOES IT HELP YOU TO HAVE ENEMIES?

WHO ARE THE GHOSTS THAT HAUNT YOU? AND WHY?

Take into consideration that it could be the ghost of a younger you.

15

WHAT DO YOU HOPE FOR?

HOW WOULD YOU DEFINE THE DIFFERENCE BETWEEN A HOPE AND A GOAL?

WHICH OF YOUR HOPES CAN TURN INTO GOALS?

WHAT DO YOU FEAR?

CAN ANY OF YOUR FEARS TURN INTO GOALS, TOO?

It's OK if the answer to that last one is NO, of course, but if it was, come back to it later and think about it again.

ARE YOU AFRAID OF EXCESSIVE WHITE SPACE?

OR ARE YOU MORE AFRAID OF WIDOWS?

Or teeny-tiny type?

Boo!

WHAT 10 QUESTIONS DID WRITER/DIRECTOR/PRODUCER

JUDD APATOW

WISH SOMEBODY HAD ASKED HIM WHEN HE WAS A STUDENT?

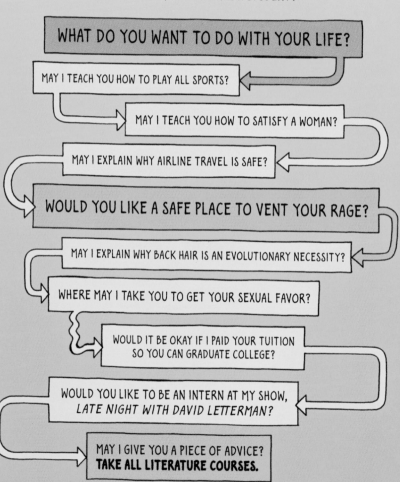

WHAT DO YOU WANT TO DO WITH YOUR LIFE?

MAY I TEACH YOU HOW TO PLAY ALL SPORTS?

MAY I TEACH YOU HOW TO SATISFY A WOMAN?

MAY I EXPLAIN WHY AIRLINE TRAVEL IS SAFE?

WOULD YOU LIKE A SAFE PLACE TO VENT YOUR RAGE?

MAY I EXPLAIN WHY BACK HAIR IS AN EVOLUTIONARY NECESSITY?

WHERE MAY I TAKE YOU TO GET YOUR SEXUAL FAVOR?

WOULD IT BE OKAY IF I PAID YOUR TUITION SO YOU CAN GRADUATE COLLEGE?

WOULD YOU LIKE TO BE AN INTERN AT MY SHOW, *LATE NIGHT WITH DAVID LETTERMAN*?

MAY I GIVE YOU A PIECE OF ADVICE? **TAKE ALL LITERATURE COURSES.**

WHAT MAKES YOU FEEL GUILTY?

WHAT MAKES YOU FEEL ASHAMED?

DOES ANYTHING IN THIS BOX HURT ANYBODY BUT YOU?

WHAT WOULD GRAPHIC DESIGNER

ARMIN VIT

LIKE TO KNOW?

HOW ARE YOU GOING TO PRESENT ALL YOUR WORK TO LOOK FOR A JOB?

HOW WOULD YOU GET THAT PRINTED?

ARE YOU READY TO TAKE DIRECTION FROM YOUR BOSS?

WHY IS THAT PRINT FILE SET UP IN RGB?

WHAT WERE YOU THINKING?

HOW ARE YOU GOING TO MAKE MONEY?

HOW WOULD YOU EXPLAIN THAT TO A CLIENT?

HAVE YOU THOUGHT ABOUT SWITCHING WEB HOSTING PROVIDERS?

DID YOU REALLY THINK THAT WAS GOING TO WORK?

CAN YOU RECOMMEND A GOOD ACCOUNTANT?

DO YOU HAVE A FILE BACK-UP SYSTEM?

DOES IT WORK ON INTERNET EXPLORER 6 ON A PC?

HAVE YOU THOUGHT ABOUT GETTING AN INTERN?

YOU WAKE UP AT 5 A.M. NOW? IT USED TO BE 5:30 A.M. ARE YOU GROWING CRAZIER?

HOW MUCH OF YOUR TIME IS DEDICATED TO FEELING BAD FOR SOMETHING YOU THINK YOU DID WRONG?

DO YOUR GUILT AND SHAME SERVE ANY USEFUL PURPOSE?

REALLY? WILL YOU PLEASE EXPLAIN THAT TO ME?

WHAT WOULD BE INVOLVED IN GETTING RID OF THAT GUILT?

COULD YOU MAKE A PHONE CALL?

OR WRITE A LETTER?

OR VISIT?

OR DO YOU HAVE TO FORGIVE YOURSELF?

CAN YOU?

CAN ANYBODY HELP YOU?

WHEN DO YOU THINK YOU'LL REACH THE POINT OF DIMINISHING RETURNS THERE?

WOULD YOU ACCEPT A FREE PASS ON THIS IF SOMEBODY GAVE IT TO YOU?

WHY NOT WRITE YOURSELF A FREE PASS RIGHT HERE?

DO YOUR GUILT AND SHAME RISE AND FALL DEPENDING ON HOW STRESSED YOU ARE?

19

CAN YOU NAME 10 THINGS THAT RELIABLY STRESS YOU OUT?

1.
2.
3.
4.
5.
6.
7.
8.
9.
10.

ON A SCALE OF 1 TO 10, HOW STRESSED ARE YOU RIGHT NOW?

1 2 3 4 5 6 7 8 9 10 11 12 13 1

DO YOU NEED 10 MORE SPACES?

1.
2.
3.
4.
5.
6.
7.
8.
9.
10.

WAS "FILLING OUT LISTS" ON YOUR LIST?

OR THE DECIMAL SYSTEM?

HOW MANY OF THESE ITEMS CAN YOU ELIMINATE THROUGH THE APPLICATION OF MONEY OR DECISIONS?

Which are renewable resources vs. your time, which is not.

DO YOU THINK STRESS IS HEROIC?

WHAT HAPPENS WHEN YOU GET STRESSED OUT?

CAN YOU PLEASE CONVINCE ME THAT THAT'S REALLY STUPID?

WHERE DID THAT IDEA START?

IN YOUR LIFE?

Yeah, I figured.

Me, too.

IN YOUR WORK?

IN YOUR BODY?

CAN YOU PLEASE DRAW A DETAILED DIAGRAM EXPLAINING THE WAYS IN WHICH YOU PROCRASTINATE?

CAN YOU NAME 10 OTHER THINGS YOU DO TO PROCRASTINATE?

1.
2.
3.
4.
5.
6.
7.
8.
9.
10.

WHAT THINGS DO YOU DO THAT YOU'VE CONVINCED YOURSELF AREN'T REALLY PROCRASTINATION?

WHAT WOULD PHOTOGRAPHER AND DIRECTOR

JONA FRANK

LIKE TO KNOW?

ARE YOU CLEAR ABOUT WHAT YOU WANT TO GET DONE?

HAVE YOU WRITTEN IT DOWN?

HAVE YOU MADE A REALISTIC LIST FOR THE DAY?

DO YOU KNOW HOW FAR YOU WANT TO GET TODAY—NOT LONG TERM, BUT SHORT TERM. DO YOU HAVE A PLAN TO COMPLETE IT?

WHAT CAN YOU DO / ACHIEVE / BEGIN TODAY?

WHAT'S MORE IMPORTANT?

YOUR WORK?   WATCHING TV?

FOLDING THAT LAUNDRY?

AND THE 10 EXCUSES YOU MAKE TO JUSTIFY YOUR PROCRASTINATION?

1.
2.
3.
4.
5.
6.
7.
8.
9.
10.

SEE WHAT I'M DOING THERE?

YOU'RE PROCRASTINATING RIGHT NOW, AREN'T YOU?

Don't be ashamed. Remember pages 18 and 19. We all do it. I know I do. So many hours of *Law & Order*.

WHO'S YOUR FAVORITE ASST. D.A.?

DO YOU REALLY NEED TO MEET THAT PERSON RIGHT NOW?

HOW IS HE/SHE GOING TO HELP YOU ACHIEVE YOUR PURPOSE TODAY?

IF THEY ARE NOT, WHY NOT SKIP THE MEETING, MAKE YOUR BED (COMPLETE **SOMETHING!**) AND GET TO WORK?

BUT, ASK YOURSELF: CAN THE LAUNDRY WAIT? CAN YOU RUN THAT ERRAND TOMORROW?

IN FACT, DO YOU HAVE ONE AFTERNOON A WEEK WHEN YOU CAN RUN THOSE ERRANDS *AND* MEET THAT FRIEND?

DO YOU HAVE A TIME OF DAY WHEN YOU ARE MOST CREATIVE, MOST ALERT?

WHEN YOU FIGURE OUT THAT TIME, WILL YOU CLOSE THE DOOR AND ACTUALLY USE IT?

DO YOU HAVE A BALANCE BETWEEN WORK AND FUN?

WHAT IS PREVENTING YOU FROM FOCUSING?

DO YOU REALLY NEED TO CHECK YOUR E-MAIL AGAIN?

DO YOU REALLY NEED ANOTHER LATTE?

WHAT ELSE DO YOU DO TO SABOTAGE YOURSELF?

WHAT THINGS DO YOU TELL YOURSELF
THAT YOU WOULD NEVER LET SOMEBODY
ELSE SAY TO YOU?

OR HAVE YOU PERFECTED
A TECHNIQUE OF GETTING
OTHER PEOPLE TO KEEP YOU
DOWN SO YOU CAN TELL
YOURSELF IT'S NOT YOU?

Oh yes! The smaller the type,
the tougher the love.

Why do you squint your eyes like that?
You'll get wrinkles. And nobody will love you
with a face full of wrinkles.

OK. That wasn't tough love. That was
just dickish. And untrue. Still, you might
invest in a loupe for the tiniest type.

ARE YOU AFRAID OF REACHING YOUR GOALS?

WHY? WHAT DO YOU THINK SUCCESS WILL MEAN?

DO YOU THINK YOU DESERVE TO REACH YOUR GOALS?

HOW DO YOU KNOW WHAT'S REAL?

YOUR MOST OPTIMISTIC VIEW?

YOUR DOOMSDAY SCENARIO?

WOULD YOU AGREE THAT "SOMEWHERE IN THE MIDDLE" IS AN OBVIOUS AND PATRONIZING ANSWER?

SPEAKING OF PATRONIZING, WOULD YOU PLEASE LIST THE INSTANCES WHERE THINGS GOT TO BE AS BAD AS YOU FEARED, OR EVEN WORSE?

HOW DID YOU GET OUT OF THOSE SITUATIONS?

WHAT DID YOU GET OUT OF THOSE SITUATIONS?

CAN YOU MAKE THE DECISION?

AT WHAT POINT DO YOU NEED OTHER PEOPLE TO SUPPORT THE DECISIONS YOU'VE MADE ABOUT YOUR OWN REALITY?

WITH THEIR BELIEF? → WITH THEIR ACTIONS?

WITH THEIR CHECK BOOK? → WITH PROPER INTRODUCTIONS?

WITH FREE BABY-SITTING?

HOW DOES YOUR IMAGE OF REALITY INTERSECT WITH THEIRS?

DOES IT MATTER? → TO YOU?

TO THEM?

WHAT ARE YOUR AMBITIONS?

DO YOU WANT TO BE RICH?

DO YOU WANT TO BE THE BEST AT WHAT YOU DO?

DO YOU WANT TO BE FAMOUS?

WHY?

DO YOU WANT TO BE A HERO?

DO YOU WANT TO SAVE PEOPLE?

DO YOU WANT TO PROVE SOMETHING?

WHAT DO YOU DO IF YOU REALIZE YOUR AMBITION WITH TIME TO SPARE?

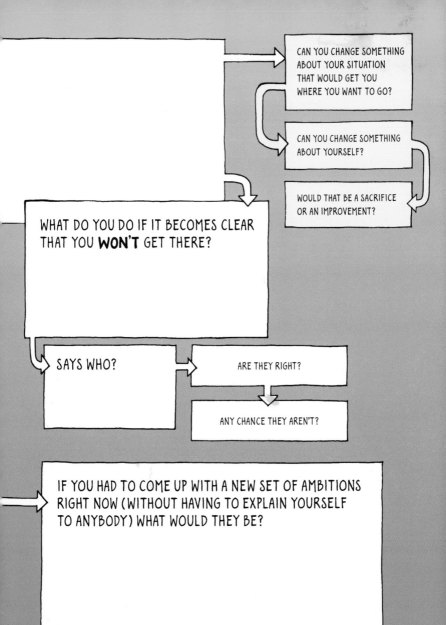

CAN YOU CHANGE SOMETHING ABOUT YOUR SITUATION THAT WOULD GET YOU WHERE YOU WANT TO GO?

CAN YOU CHANGE SOMETHING ABOUT YOURSELF?

WOULD THAT BE A SACRIFICE OR AN IMPROVEMENT?

WHAT DO YOU DO IF IT BECOMES CLEAR THAT YOU **WON'T** GET THERE?

SAYS WHO?

ARE THEY RIGHT?

ANY CHANCE THEY AREN'T?

IF YOU HAD TO COME UP WITH A NEW SET OF AMBITIONS RIGHT NOW (WITHOUT HAVING TO EXPLAIN YOURSELF TO ANYBODY) WHAT WOULD THEY BE?

HOW ARE YOU EDUCATING YOURSELF?

WHAT PRICE ARE YOU PAYING FOR YOUR EDUCATION?

HOW DO YOU CHOOSE YOUR TEACHERS?

ARE YOU INTIMIDATED BY YOUR FELLOW STUDENTS?

WHY THE HELL NOT?

WHERE WILL YOU FIND PEOPLE THAT INTIMIDATE YOU?

OR WOULD YOU RATHER THAT PEOPLE BE INTIMIDATED BY YOU?

WHAT WOULD YOU LEARN FROM THAT?

ZE FRANK

IF YOU HAD TO GRADE YOURSELF IN EACH OF YOUR CLASSES, WHAT GRADE WOULD YOU GET?

WHAT RESOURCES ARE YOU NOT TAKING ADVANTAGE OF?

WHAT QUESTIONS DO YOU HAVE ABOUT YOUR FIRST COUPLE OF YEARS AFTER SCHOOL ENDS?

ARE YOU TAKING RISKS TOWARDS CREATING FRIENDSHIPS?

WHAT DO YOU KNOW ABOUT THE GEOGRAPHICAL PLACE YOU ARE IN?

WHEN YOU DON'T UNDERSTAND SOMETHING ARE YOU IMMEDIATELY ASKING QUESTIONS?

IF YOU THOUGHT OF YOUR FRIENDS AS A COLLECTION, WHAT IS THE MOST DOMINANT ATTRIBUTE THAT YOU SEEM TO BE COLLECTING?

ARE YOU ASKING ENOUGH QUESTIONS?

ARE YOU AIMING ANY **CREATIVE** ENERGY AT UNDERSTANDING YOURSELF?

WHY WOULD YOU DO ANYTHING HALF WAY?

REMEMBER PAGES 10 AND 11? HAVE YOU HAD ANY ADDITIONAL THOUGHTS ON THAT?

WHAT DO YOU REALLY ACTUALLY WANT?

ARE YOU ON THE RIGHT PATH TO GET THERE?

IN AN IDEAL WORLD, WHAT WOULD BE THE FASTEST, MOST DIRECT WAY OF GETTING THERE?

WHAT WOULD BE THE MOST INTERESTING WAY?

WHAT WOULD BE THE MOST FUN WAY?

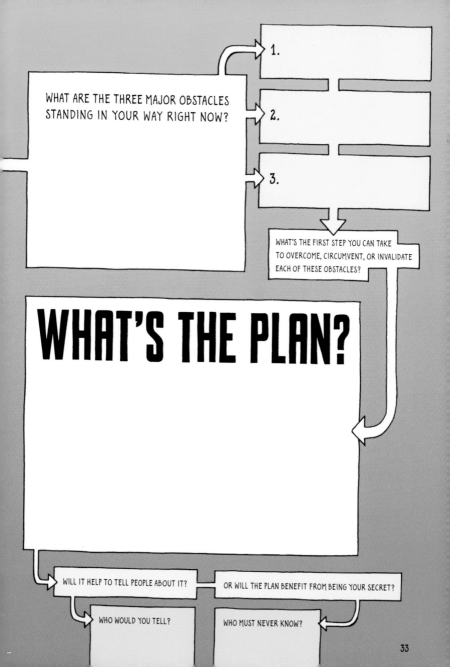

WHAT ARE THE THREE MAJOR OBSTACLES STANDING IN YOUR WAY RIGHT NOW?

1.

2.

3.

WHAT'S THE FIRST STEP YOU CAN TAKE TO OVERCOME, CIRCUMVENT, OR INVALIDATE EACH OF THESE OBSTACLES?

WHAT'S THE PLAN?

WILL IT HELP TO TELL PEOPLE ABOUT IT?

OR WILL THE PLAN BENEFIT FROM BEING YOUR SECRET?

WHO WOULD YOU TELL?

WHO MUST NEVER KNOW?

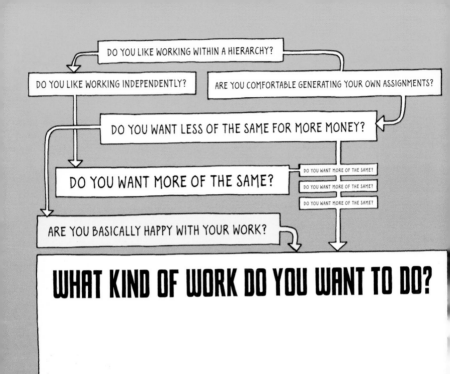

DO YOU LIKE WORKING WITHIN A HIERARCHY?

DO YOU LIKE WORKING INDEPENDENTLY?

ARE YOU COMFORTABLE GENERATING YOUR OWN ASSIGNMENTS?

DO YOU WANT LESS OF THE SAME FOR MORE MONEY?

DO YOU WANT MORE OF THE SAME?

DO YOU WANT MORE OF THE SAME?
DO YOU WANT MORE OF THE SAME?
DO YOU WANT MORE OF THE SAME?

ARE YOU BASICALLY HAPPY WITH YOUR WORK?

WHAT KIND OF WORK DO YOU WANT TO DO?

ARE YOU LOOKING FOR A RADICAL SHIFT?

ARE YOU LOOKING FOR AN EVOLUTION?

WHAT ARE THE FIVE HALLMARKS OF YOUR IDEAL JOB?

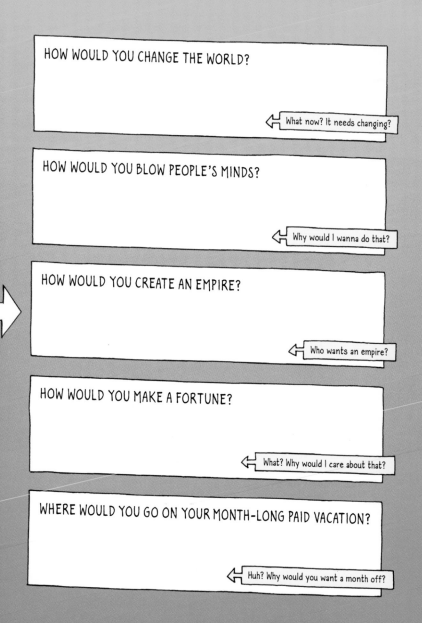

HOW WOULD YOU CHANGE THE WORLD?

What now? It needs changing?

HOW WOULD YOU BLOW PEOPLE'S MINDS?

Why would I wanna do that?

HOW WOULD YOU CREATE AN EMPIRE?

Who wants an empire?

HOW WOULD YOU MAKE A FORTUNE?

What? Why would I care about that?

WHERE WOULD YOU GO ON YOUR MONTH-LONG PAID VACATION?

Huh? Why would you want a month off?

WHAT DISTINGUISHES A GOOD IDEA
FROM A BAD IDEA?

DO YOU HAVE WAY TOO MANY IDEAS
TO CHOOSE FROM ALL THE TIME?

DO YOU HAVE LOTS OF IDEAS TO CHOOSE FROM
WHEN YOU NEED THEM?

DO YOU NEED INSPIRATION?

DO YOU FIND YOURSELF AT A LOSS FOR IDEAS
WHEN THE PRESSURE IS ON?

DO YOU FIND YOURSELF AT A LOSS FOR IDEAS
WHEN THE PRESSURE IS OFF?

DO YOU PREFER PERFECTING WHAT YOU DO
BY DOING IT OVER AND OVER FOR YEARS
UNTIL YOU GET IT RIGHT?

ARE YOU RESPONSIBLE FOR YOUR IDEAS?

OR DO YOU LIKE TO BOUNCE AROUND,
TRYING NEW THINGS ALL THE TIME?

ARE YOU RESPONSIBLE **TO** YOUR IDEAS?

WHAT ARE SOME OF THE IDEAS YOU'VE HAD OVER THE YEARS
THAT YOU NEVER GOT TO MAKE REAL?

WHICH ONE HAUNTS YOU MOST?

WHAT CAN YOU DO RIGHT NOW
TO BRING THAT ONE BACK TO LIFE?

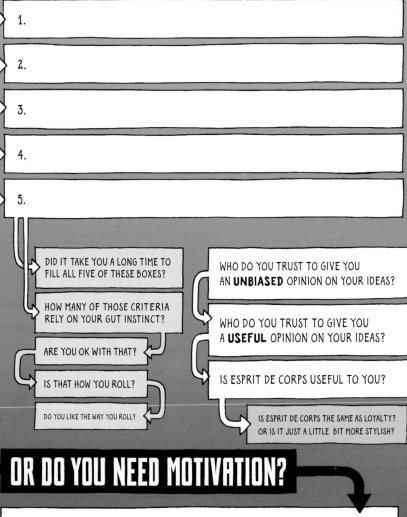

1.

2.

3.

4.

5.

DID IT TAKE YOU A LONG TIME TO FILL ALL FIVE OF THESE BOXES?

HOW MANY OF THOSE CRITERIA RELY ON YOUR GUT INSTINCT?

ARE YOU OK WITH THAT?

IS THAT HOW YOU ROLL?

DO YOU LIKE THE WAY YOU ROLL?

WHO DO YOU TRUST TO GIVE YOU AN **UNBIASED** OPINION ON YOUR IDEAS?

WHO DO YOU TRUST TO GIVE YOU A **USEFUL** OPINION ON YOUR IDEAS?

IS ESPRIT DE CORPS USEFUL TO YOU?

IS ESPRIT DE CORPS THE SAME AS LOYALTY? OR IS IT JUST A LITTLE BIT MORE STYLISH?

OR DO YOU NEED MOTIVATION?

WHAT **WOULD** MOTIVATE YOU TO GET TO WORK?

IN TERMS OF YOUR WORK, WHAT ARE THE MOST TIME- AND COST-EFFICIENT WAYS TO HAVE FUN?

HAVE THEY YIELDED USEFUL RESULTS?

HOW USEFUL IS FUN?

ON A SCALE OF 1 THROUGH YES?

HAVE YOU EXPERIMENTED WITH ALTERED STATES?

HAVE THEY BEEN FUN?

WHAT ARE THE PLACES WHERE IDEAS COME TO YOU MORE READILY?

WHAT DO YOU DO TO GET INSPIRED?

WHO DOES WHAT YOU WANT TO DO, OR DOES WHAT YOU ALREADY DO, JUST MUCH BETTER?

ARE THEY INSPIRING TO YOU? OR FRUSTRATING? OR BOTH?

WHERE DO YOU DRAW THE LINE BETWEEN INSPIRATION AND IMITATION?

WHAT WOULD **THE COLBERT REPORT** WRITER

MEREDITH SCARDINO

LIKE TO KNOW?

ARE YOU WILLING TO PLAGIARIZE?

MANY OF THE GREATEST WRITERS AND THINKERS SUFFERED CRIPPLING ADDICTIONS. WHAT WILL BE YOUR DRUG/INDUSTRIAL SOLVENT OF CHOICE?

WHICH OF YOUR CHILDHOOD PETS HAD THE BEST IDEAS?

A GREAT ARTIST CAN GET INSPIRATION FROM ANYWHERE. WHAT INSPIRES YOU AT FUNERALS, DOG FIGHTS, AND HIGHWAY CAR WRECKS?

WHICH HAD THE WORST?

LET'S BUILD YOUR SELF-ESTEEM. THINK OF A NUMBER BETWEEN 1 AND 10. NOW CAN YOU GUESS WHAT NUMBER YOU WERE THINKING OF?

WHERE DO YOU SEE YOURSELF IN 5 YEARS? 10 YEARS? 200?

LOOK IN THE MIRROR, WHAT DO YOU SEE? (FEEL FREE TO INCLUDE AND CHART SUSPICIOUS MOLES.)

WAS THIS BOOK WORTH $14.99? (OR IF IT WAS A GIFT, WAS IT WORTH THE $150 YOUR VERY THOUGHTFUL FRIEND PAID?)

WHAT ARE YOUR INSECURITIES?

I bet it's your weird laugh everyone talks about when you're not around.

ARE YOU COMMITTED TO FOLLOWING YOUR DREAMS?

WHAT IS HEARSAY?

EVEN THAT ONE WHERE YOU HAD A LION BODY AND DID THAT THING WITH YOUR OLD LATIN TEACHER?

WHO IS HENRY VIII?

WHAT IS ANDROMEDA?

CAN YOU TAKE CRITICISM? FIND OUT BY LISTING WHAT YOU HATE MOST ABOUT YOURSELF.

ARE THOSE QUESTIONS TO SPARK CREATIVITY OR JUST LIFTED FROM JEOPARDY?

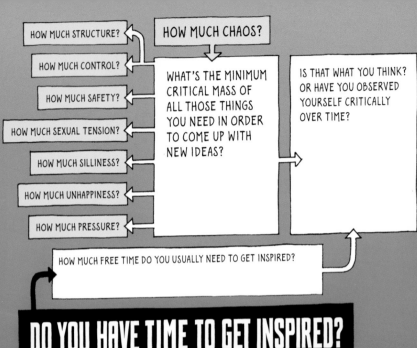

HOW MUCH CHAOS?

HOW MUCH STRUCTURE?

HOW MUCH CONTROL?

HOW MUCH SAFETY?

HOW MUCH SEXUAL TENSION?

HOW MUCH SILLINESS?

HOW MUCH UNHAPPINESS?

HOW MUCH PRESSURE?

WHAT'S THE MINIMUM CRITICAL MASS OF ALL THOSE THINGS YOU NEED IN ORDER TO COME UP WITH NEW IDEAS?

IS THAT WHAT YOU THINK? OR HAVE YOU OBSERVED YOURSELF CRITICALLY OVER TIME?

HOW MUCH FREE TIME DO YOU USUALLY NEED TO GET INSPIRED?

DO YOU HAVE TIME TO GET INSPIRED?

ARE THERE WAYS YOU CAN CRAM MORE INSPIRING THINGS INTO EVERYDAY ACTIVITIES?

BOOKS ON TAPE?

NPR IN THE CAR?

BOOKS ON THE TRAIN?

SING IN TIME WITH YOUR WALK?

USE THE CURB AS A BALANCE BEAM?

ARRANGE EVERYTHING ON YOUR DESK BY COLOR?

CARVE GOOGLY EYES INTO YOUR FRUITS & VEGETABLES?

FOLD YOUR JUNK MAIL INTO PAPER CRANES?

CAN YOU SCHEDULE 15 MINUTES EVERY DAY THIS WEEK TO WRITE DOWN IDEAS?

MONDAY	TUESDAY	WEDNESDAY	THURSDAY	FRIDAY	SATURDAY	SUNDAY

DO YOU KNOW WHEN TO SAY "ENOUGH" AND MOVE FROM INSPIRATION TO DOING THE WORK AT HAND?

CAN YOU SCHEDULE AN EXTRA 15 MINUTES AT THE END OF THE WEEK TO GO OVER WHAT YOU'VE COME UP WITH?

DO YOU THINK INSPIRATION ONLY TRULY STRIKES WHEN YOU GET TO WORK ANYWAY?

DO YOU CLAIM YOUR SHOWER AS A HOME OFFICE ON YOUR TAX RETURN?

HAVE YOU MADE TIME TO SIMPLY REST?

DO YOU BELIEVE IN THE WISDOM OF LETTING YOUR FIELDS LAY FALLOW NOW AND AGAIN?

SO YOU'RE INSPIRED NOW?
WELL? WHADAYA GONNA DO ABOUT IT?

DO YOU HAVE A WORKING SYSTEM TO FIND IDEAS AGAIN AFTER TIME HAS PASSED?

HOW DO YOU RECORD YOUR IDEAS?

HOW DO YOU PRIORITIZE YOUR IDEAS?

WHAT DO YOU ENJOY MORE:
TALKING ABOUT YOUR IDEAS WITH OTHERS,
OR DEVELOPING THEM IN SECRET??

WHEN IS THE MOST EFFECTIVE TIME FOR YOU
TO LET OTHER PEOPLE IN ON YOUR IDEAS?

WHO CAN HELP YOU
MAKE YOUR IDEAS REAL?

WHAT'S IN IT FOR THEM?

DAVE STEWART

LIKE TO KNOW?

WHAT DO YOU THINK ABOUT WHEN YOU FIRST WAKE UP?

HOW SOON CAN YOU FORGET A MEETING ONCE IT'S OVER KNOWING NOTES WERE TAKEN AND DECISIONS MADE?

HOW LONG DO YOU HANG ON TO AN IDEA WHEN IN THE BACK OF YOUR MIND YOU KNOW IT'S PAST ITS DUE DATE?

DO YOU GET MORE INTERESTING IDEAS TALKING TO OTHER ARTISTS OR TO OTHER ENTREPRENEURS?

HOW SOON DO YOU TELL PEOPLE THAT YOU ARE NOT ON THE SAME WAVE LENGTH?

HOW MANY TIMES HAVE YOU SAID
"I DON'T UNDERSTAND"
WITH EAGERNESS?

HOW DO YOU RECORD YOUR IDEAS?

HOW MANY PEOPLE CAN YOU TALK IN SHORTHAND WITH?

WHO WOULD BE YOUR BEST IDEA ARCHIVIST?

HOW LONG DO YOU TAKE TO GET

IF YOU WORKED IN A HOSPITAL WHAT WOULD BE THE ROLE YOU WOULD CHOOSE?

WHAT IS SEXY ABOUT YOUR LIFE?

WHAT IS SEXY ABOUT YOUR WORK?

HOW MANY TIMES HAVE YOU SEEN YOUR IDEA ALREADY OUT THERE?

TO THE POINT?

DO YOU NEED

WHOSE PERMISSION DO YOU NEED TO DO WHAT YOU WANT TO DO?

WHOSE PERMISSION DO YOU SEEK?

YOUR PARENTS? → YOUR PARTNER? → YOUR KIDS?

THE HEAD OF YOUR CRIME SYNDICATE? ← YOUR BANK?

THE GOVERNMENT? → YOUR LANDLORD? → YOUR GOD?

WHO WILL PUNISH YOU IF YOU DON'T GET THEIR APPROVAL BEFORE YOU PROCEED?

WHOSE LIFE WILL BE AFFECTED BY YOUR PLANS?

WHEN IS SOMEBODY ELSE'S DISAPPROVAL OR DISAPPOINTMENT WORSE THAN SHELVING AN IDEA?

HOW OFTEN HAVE YOU TAKEN AN OLD IDEA OFF THE SHELF AND MADE IT HAPPEN?

PERMISSION?

DO YOU SEEK PERMISSION TO RECEIVE ENCOURAGEMENT OR TO AVOID PENALTY?

WHOSE PERMISSION IS NO LONGER AVAILABLE TO YOU?

DO YOU THINK THEY WOULD HAVE GIVEN IT?

DOES THAT THOUGHT SPUR YOU ON EITHER WAY?

SAY YOU HAVE AN IDEA OR A PLAN FOR YOUR LIFE THAT'S SO GREAT THAT IT BURNS IN YOUR BRAIN EVERY DAY, THAT'S SO OBVIOUSLY EXCELLENT THAT YOU HAVE NO DOUBT IT'S WORTH EVERY DROP OF ENERGY YOU CAN GIVE IT — DO YOU STILL FEEL LIKE YOU NEED PERMISSION? EVEN IF IT'S JUST FOR PARTS OF IT?

CAN YOU KEEP MOVING WITHOUT PERMISSION?

WHEN IS IT BETTER TO ASK FOR FORGIVENESS THAN PERMISSION?

WHEN IS ASKING FOR FORGIVENESS AN UNFAIR MOVE?

Who decides—how?

DO YOU NEED PATRONS?

DO YOU NEED CLIENTS? → HOW MANY CLIENTS DO YOU NEED?

DO YOU NEED AN EMPLOYER TO DO WHAT YOU WANT TO DO?

WHAT KIND OF POWER DO YOU NEED TO DO WHAT YOU WANT TO DO?

WHAT WILL YOU GIVE UP IN EXCHANGE FOR THIS POWER?

WILL FINANCIAL AND PROCEDURAL STABILITY FREE YOUR MIND TO EVOLVE
TO THE NEXT STAGE, OR WILL A DAILY ROUTINE OCCUPY TOO MUCH
OF YOUR TIME?

HOW MUCH OF YOUR OWN MONEY ARE YOU WILLING TO RISK
AS YOU GO WHERE YOU WANT TO GO?

WHAT DO YOU DO IF YOU HAVE NO MONEY OF YOUR OWN TO RISK?

HOW MUCH MONEY IN THE BANK DOES IT TAKE FOR YOU TO FEEL SAFE?

WHAT WOULD AUTHOR, COLUMNIST, AND ADVERTISING PERSON

RUSSELL M. DAVIES

LIKE TO KNOW?

GIVEN MEDICAL ADVANCES AND REDUCING PENSIONS YOUR WORKING LIFE IS LIKELY TO LAST MORE THAN 100 YEARS, WHAT ARE YOU DOING TO PREPARE FOR THAT?

HOW MUCH OF YOUR DAY WOULD YOU LIKE TO SPEND LAUGHING?

HAVE YOU LEARNED TO DRAW YET?

WOULDN'T YOU LEARN MORE BY GETTING A JOB?

HOW, EXACTLY, DO YOU THINK GRAVITY WORKS?

WHAT DO YOU REALLY, REALLY LIKE DOING? SHOULDN'T YOU BE DOING THAT?

WHEN ARE YOU MOST PRODUCTIVE — MORNING OR AFTERNOON?

YOU KNOW HOW THE INTERNET OVERTURNED PROFESSIONS LIKE PHOTOGRAPHY AND MUSIC— WHAT WILL YOU DO WHEN IT DOES IT TO YOU?

WHEN ARE YOU MOST PRODUCTIVE — WINTER OR SUMMER?

WHEN ARE YOU GOING TO STOP DRESSING LIKE A TEENAGER?

HOW SOON BEFORE YOU'RE REPLACED BY A ROBOT?

HOW SOON BEFORE YOU **ARE** A ROBOT?

WHAT DOES THE PHRASE 'SEMI-LIVING WORRY-DOLL' MEAN TO YOU?

DO YOU REALLY NEED TO BE HERE THIS LATE?

ISN'T IT TIME TO STOP COASTING AND MAKE SOMETHING NEW?

DO YOU REALLY NEED TO EAT ALL THOSE CHIPS?

HOW, EXACTLY, DO YOU THINK YOU WORK?

IF YOU WENT BACK IN TIME 100 YEARS WHAT COULD YOU SAY TO ANYONE THAT WOULD BE USEFUL OR HELPFUL IN ANY WAY?

WHEN ARE YOU HAPPIEST? TO THE MINUTE?

WHO ARE YOU TRYING TO IMPRESS?

WHAT WILL YOU BE DOING WITH THE NEXT 60 YEARS?

likely chewing before they're up. –

WHAT'S THE FIRST STEP?

ARE YOU THINKING TOO BIG?

ARE YOU THINKING TOO FAST?

WHAT'S THE FIRST STEP OF THE FIRST STEP?

WHAT CAN YOU DO RIGHT THIS MINUTE?

WHAT WILL YOU DO BEFORE THE END OF TODAY?

WHAT WILL YOU DO BEFORE THE END OF THIS WEEK?

HOW WILL YOU FEEL UNTIL YOU TAKE THAT FIRST STEP?

HOW WILL YOU FEEL WHEN YOU DO?

AT WHAT POINT WILL CHANGING THINGS BECOME RISKY FOR YOU?

RISKY TO YOUR LIVELIHOOD?

WHAT WILL HAPPEN IF YOU FAIL?

RISKY FOR YOUR FAMILY'S LIVELIHOOD?

RISKY FOR YOUR REPUTATION?

RISKY FOR YOUR RECORD OF ACCOMPLISHMENT?

RISKY FOR YOUR SENSE OF ACCOMPLISHMENT?

RISKY FOR YOUR PRIDE?

ARE YOU READY TO MOVE ALREADY?

WHAT HAPPENED LAST TIME YOU FAILED?

WHAT MAKES YOU FEEL TRAPPED?

HOW DO YOU DEFINE FREEDOM?

WHAT MAKES YOU FEEL FREE?

WHAT ARE THE FIVE EASIEST THINGS YOU CAN DO TO INCREASE YOUR FREEDOM?

WHAT ARE THE FIVE MOST DIFFICULT THINGS?

WHAT ARE FIVE FREEDOMS YOU ALREADY HAVE BUT DON'T USE?

DO YOU PREFER STABILITY OVER FREEDOM?

DOES MONEY EQUAL STABILITY?

DOES MONEY EQUAL FREEDOM?

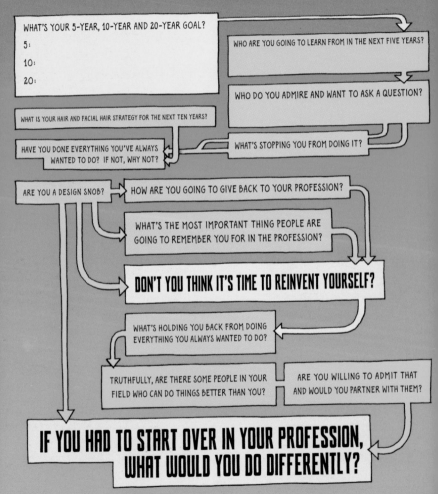

WHAT WOULD DESIGNER

STANLEY HAINSWORTH

LIKE TO KNOW?

WHAT'S YOUR 5-YEAR, 10-YEAR AND 20-YEAR GOAL?

5:

10:

20:

WHO ARE YOU GOING TO LEARN FROM IN THE NEXT FIVE YEARS?

WHO DO YOU ADMIRE AND WANT TO ASK A QUESTION?

WHAT IS YOUR HAIR AND FACIAL HAIR STRATEGY FOR THE NEXT TEN YEARS?

HAVE YOU DONE EVERYTHING YOU'VE ALWAYS WANTED TO DO? IF NOT, WHY NOT?

WHAT'S STOPPING YOU FROM DOING IT?

ARE YOU A DESIGN SNOB?

HOW ARE YOU GOING TO GIVE BACK TO YOUR PROFESSION?

WHAT'S THE MOST IMPORTANT THING PEOPLE ARE GOING TO REMEMBER YOU FOR IN THE PROFESSION?

DON'T YOU THINK IT'S TIME TO REINVENT YOURSELF?

WHAT'S HOLDING YOU BACK FROM DOING EVERYTHING YOU ALWAYS WANTED TO DO?

TRUTHFULLY, ARE THERE SOME PEOPLE IN YOUR FIELD WHO CAN DO THINGS BETTER THAN YOU?

ARE YOU WILLING TO ADMIT THAT AND WOULD YOU PARTNER WITH THEM?

IF YOU HAD TO START OVER IN YOUR PROFESSION, WHAT WOULD YOU DO DIFFERENTLY?

HOW MUCH CAN YOU WHORE YOURSELF OUT?

WHAT KIND OF PEOPLE DO YOU LIKE TO WORK WITH?

DO YOU WANT TO MAKE MONEY?

DO YOU WANT TO COLLABORATE ON EVERY PROJECT?

HOW MUCH MONEY?

CAN YOU DEAL WITH MULTIPLE PERSONALITY TYPES?

CAN YOU SUFFER FOOLS?

ARE YOU WILLING TO BE TREATED LIKE AN EXOTIC MENIAL SERVANT?

WHAT QUESTIONS DOES DESIGNER

SEAN ADAMS

WISH HE'D BEEN ASKED AS A STUDENT, AND A YEAR AGO?

WILL YOU MIND IF I START TREATING YOU LIKE A PROFESSIONAL?

WOULD YOU LIKE FAME TO TRANSLATE INTO MONEY?

WOULD YOU LIKE A BIG BUDGET AND LOTS OF TIME?

HOW BIG

HOW SMALL CAN YOU BE?

TO BE MOST EFFECTIVE?

WHICH OF THE FOLLOWING ATTRIBUTES WOULD MAKE THE MOST POWERFUL COMBINATION IN YOUR SITUATION?

YOUNG
ESTABLISHED
EXPERIENCED
POWERFUL
INNOVATIVE
QUIRKY
NIMBLE
UNTIRING
FUNNY
INSIGHTFUL
RESPONSIVE
RESPONSIBLE
PREDICTABLE

WHAT ARE THE ADVANTAGES OF MAKING YOURSELF LOOK LIKE A BIG COMPANY?

WHAT ARE THE ADVANTAGES OF MAKING YOURSELF LOOK LIKE AN INDIE UPSTART?

CAN YOU BE?

HOW WOULD YOUR WORK CHANGE IF YOU PRETENDED (TO YOURSELF) THAT YOU'VE ALREADY ACHIEVED ALL OF YOUR PROFESSIONAL GOALS?

WHAT WILL MAKE PEOPLE THINK THEY'RE DEALING WITH A **BIG FIRM?**

WHAT WILL MAKE PEOPLE FEEL THAT THEY'RE DEALING WITH A **FRESH, YOUNG VOICE?**

HOW WILL THE WAY YOU PRESENT YOURSELF AFFECT THE WORK YOU DO OR HOW YOU DO IT?

WILL THAT CHANGE BE VISIBLE TO OTHERS?

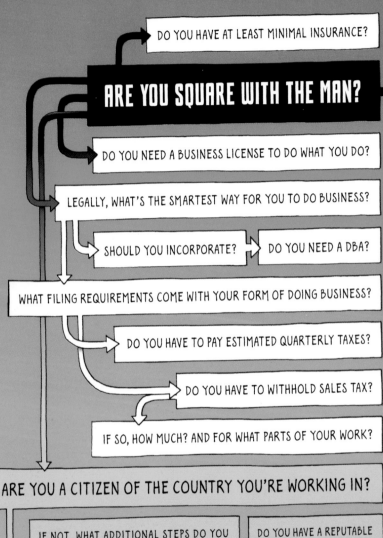

DO YOU HAVE AT LEAST MINIMAL INSURANCE?

ARE YOU SQUARE WITH THE MAN?

DO YOU NEED A BUSINESS LICENSE TO DO WHAT YOU DO?

LEGALLY, WHAT'S THE SMARTEST WAY FOR YOU TO DO BUSINESS?

SHOULD YOU INCORPORATE?

DO YOU NEED A DBA?

WHAT FILING REQUIREMENTS COME WITH YOUR FORM OF DOING BUSINESS?

DO YOU HAVE TO PAY ESTIMATED QUARTERLY TAXES?

DO YOU HAVE TO WITHHOLD SALES TAX?

IF SO, HOW MUCH? AND FOR WHAT PARTS OF YOUR WORK?

ARE YOU A CITIZEN OF THE COUNTRY YOU'RE WORKING IN?

IF NOT, WHAT ADDITIONAL STEPS DO YOU HAVE TO TAKE TO COMPLY WITH GOVERNMENT REGULATIONS NOW AND IN THE FUTURE?

DO YOU HAVE A REPUTABLE IMMIGRATION ATTORNEY?

56

DO YOU HAVE AN ACCOUNTANT?

DO YOU HAVE AN ATTORNEY?

OR DO YOU HAVE TRUSTED ADVISORS THAT CAN TAKE THEIR PLACE?

HOW DO YOU KNOW YOU CAN TRUST THEIR ADVICE?

WOULD YOU LISTEN TO A TRUSTED ADVISOR OVER YOUR DOCTOR?

ARE YOU A GAMBLER? → ARE YOU A CYNIC?

HAVE YOU HEARD THE SAYING "A STITCH IN TIME SAVES NINE"?

HOW MUCH TIME, MONEY, AND CREATIVE ENERGY WILL IT COST YOU IF YOU GET AUDITED, HAVE TO PAY FINES, PENALTIES, AND LATE FEES BECAUSE OF INSUFFICIENT PLANNING OR SHODDY PAPERWORK?

HOW MUCH IS YOUR MENTAL BANDWIDTH WORTH?

ARE YOU GOOD AT TALKING ABOUT YOUR WORK?

ARE YOU GOOD AT TALKING ABOUT YOUR WORK TO COLLEAGUES?

ARE YOU GOOD AT TALKING ABOUT YOUR WORK TO POSSIBLE CLIENTS, EMPLOYERS, OR PATRONS?

HOW WILL YOU BECOME A BETTER REPRESENTATIVE FOR YOURSELF?

HOW DO YOU FIND WORK?

ARE YOU SHOWING YOUR WORK IN ITS BEST LIGHT?

ARE YOU SHOWING YOURSELF IN YOUR BEST LIGHT?

HOW MUCH TIME, EFFORT, AND MONEY HAVE YOU INVESTED IN PRESENTING YOURSELF AND YOUR WORK BEAUTIFULLY?

WHAT ARE FIVE THINGS YOU CAN DO TO IMPROVE HOW PEOPLE SEE WHAT YOU CAN DO?

ARE YOU, IN FACT, THE BEST PERSON TO REPRESENT YOUR WORK?

IS THERE SOMEBODY BETTER? → A TRAINED PROFESSIONAL?

A BUSINESS PARTNER?

HOW DO YOU ATTRACT **THAT** PERSON?

ARE YOU COMFORTABLE MAKING COLD CALLS?

DO YOU HAVE FRIENDS WHO'LL PRACTICE WITH YOU?

HAVE YOU ASKED YOUR FRIENDS AND FAMILY FOR LEADS?

DO YOU THINK YOU'D FEEL QUEASY AND VAGUELY DIRTY IF YOU DID?

HAVE FRIENDS OR RELATIVES EVER ASKED YOU FOR LEADS?

WAS IT A BIG DEAL EITHER WAY?

DO YOU THINK WINNING AWARDS WILL LEAD TO WORK?

DO YOU THINK THE WORK SHOULD SPEAK FOR ITSELF?

DO YOU REALIZE THAT I AGREE WITH YOU?

YOU DO REALIZE WE'RE BOTH WRONG, RIGHT?

WHAT ARE THE FIVE THINGS THAT ARE MOST IMPORTANT TO YOU IN THE WORK YOU PRODUCE?

HOW DO YOU DEFINE INTEGRITY?

WHAT ARE THE FIVE THINGS THAT ARE MOST IMPORTANT TO YOU IN THE WAY YOU DEAL WITH THE PEOPLE IN YOUR LIFE?

WHAT WOULD **FLAMING LIPS** FRONTMAN

WAYNE COYNE

LIKE TO KNOW?

ARE ARTISTS NARCISSISTIC ASSHOLES ... ????

SHOULD ARTISTS CARE ABOUT MONEY ... ??

IS COMPLETE FREEDOM WHAT ARTISTS REALLY WANT ... ???

WHY IS PAIN AND FEAR THE DRIVING FORCE BEHIND MOST ART ... ???

WHAT IS MORE IMPORTANT—STICKING TO YOUR CONVICTIONS OR MAKING COMPROMISES ... ???

I'VE NOTICED SOMETIMES YOU'LL BE WORKING ON AN IDEA AND SOMETHING WILL HAPPEN AND YOU WILL QUICKLY ABANDON YOUR IDEA AND JUST GO WITH THE NEW DISCOVERY ... BUT OTHER TIMES YOU WILL KEEP FIGHTING AND FIGHTING, TRYING TO MAKE YOUR IDEA WORK ... **WHICH IS THE WAY ... ????**

HOW DO YOU TREAT YOUR COLLEAGUES DIFFERENTLY THAN YOUR FRIENDS?

HOW DO YOU TREAT CHECKERS, WAIT STAFF, AND AIRLINE EMPLOYEES?

HOW DO YOU FEEL ABOUT THOSE DIFFERENCES?

WHAT ARE THE TOP TEN THINGS ON YOUR SECRET LUXURY WISH LIST?

FANCY CAR?

FANCY SUITS?

BIG NEW TV?

BIG NEW HOUSE?

A TRIP TO THE BAHAMAS?

ORIGINAL ART BY YOUR FAVORITE PAINTER?

AN IVY LEAGUE DEGREE?

A FAMILY?

IS THAT TOO MUCH O
A HERETICAL QUESTION

ARE YOU IN CONTROL OF YOUR GREED?

WHAT'S MORE IMPORTANT TO YOU? MONEY OR FREEDOM?

DO YOU THINK THOSE ARE THE TWO SIDES OF THE EQUATION?

OR IS IT A QUADRATIC FUNCTION WHERE EARNING NO MONEY MEANS LOTS OF FREEDOM, AND LOTS OF MONEY EQUALS LOTS OF FREEDOM, BUT SOME MONEY MEANS HARDLY ANY FREEDOM AT ALL?

WHAT CAN YOU DO TO GET OUT OF THE TROUGH?

OR IS IT A TOTALLY DIFFERENT EQUATION?

CAN YOU PUT IT ON PAPER?

FREEDOM

MONEY

WHAT ARE THE TOP TEN THINGS YOU WANT TO ACHIEVE WITH YOUR WORK?

IF YOU HAD TO PUT ALL 20 OF THESE ITEMS
ON ONE MASTER LIST, HOW WOULD YOU RANK THEM?

WHAT WOULD DIRECTOR

TARSEM

LIKE TO KNOW?

WHY DOES IT LOOK LIKE YOUR VISUALS
COME BEFORE THE STORY?

WHAT DO YOU LOOK FOR IN AN ACTOR?

WHAT INTERESTS YOU IN A STORY?

HOW CLOSE DOES THE END PRODUCT
COME TO WHAT INTERESTED YOU?

IF ORIGINALITY IS THE ART
OF CONCEALING YOUR SOURCE
WHY ARE YOU DOING
SUCH A TERRIBLE JOB?

63

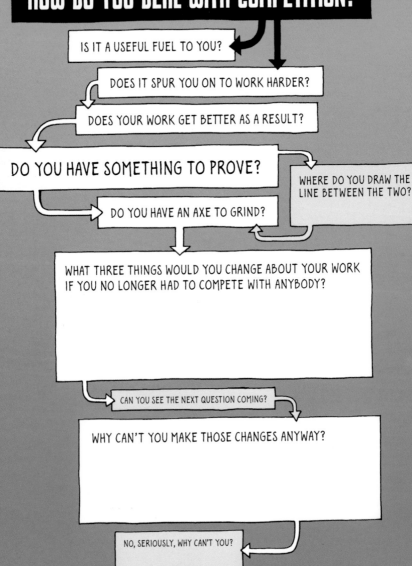

HOW DO YOU DEAL WITH COMPETITION?

IS IT A USEFUL FUEL TO YOU?

DOES IT SPUR YOU ON TO WORK HARDER?

DOES YOUR WORK GET BETTER AS A RESULT?

DO YOU HAVE SOMETHING TO PROVE?

WHERE DO YOU DRAW THE LINE BETWEEN THE TWO?

DO YOU HAVE AN AXE TO GRIND?

WHAT THREE THINGS WOULD YOU CHANGE ABOUT YOUR WORK IF YOU NO LONGER HAD TO COMPETE WITH ANYBODY?

CAN YOU SEE THE NEXT QUESTION COMING?

WHY CAN'T YOU MAKE THOSE CHANGES ANYWAY?

NO, SERIOUSLY, WHY CAN'T YOU?

WHO ARE YOUR TOP 5 COMPETITORS?

DO YOU THINK THEY WOULD CONSIDER YOU THEIR COMPETITION, TOO?

DO YOU WANT TO BE BETTER THAN THEM?

HOW WOULD YOU DEFINE "BETTER" IN THIS CONTEXT?

OR DO YOU WANT TO BEAT THEM?

WHY ARE THEY ON THE LIST?

DO YOU TAKE COMPETITION PERSONALLY?

DO YOU HATE THE PLAYER? → DO YOU HATE THE GAME?

HOW MUCH CREATIVITY DO YOU INVEST IN IMAGINING PERSONAL BATTLES ON AN AVERAGE DAY?

DOES IT LEAVE YOU INVIGORATED OR EXHAUSTED?

OR DO YOU NOT REALLY CARE ABOUT WHAT OTHER PEOPLE IN YOUR FIELD ARE UP TO?

REALLY? NOT AT ALL? WHAT'S THAT LIKE?

HAVE ANY OF YOUR COMPETITORS BECOME FRIENDS?

HOW DID THAT HAPPEN?

HOW DO YOU GET WORK APPROVED?

DO YOU WORK BASED ON STRATEGY OR INSTINCT?

CAN YOU TAKE YOUR AUDIENCE THROUGH A LINEAR THOUGHT PROCESS THAT EXPLAINS YOUR RESULTS IF NECESSARY?

CAN YOU LOOK AT YOUR WORK THROUGH THE EYES OF YOUR AUDIENCE?

CAN YOU RETURN TO YOUR OWN POINT OF VIEW AFTER YOU DO?

WHAT'S BEEN THE PROJECT THAT'S MADE BOTH YOU AND YOUR CLIENTS MOST PROUD SO FAR?

WHAT WERE THE TOP THREE THINGS THAT MADE YOU PROUD OF IT?

WHAT WERE THE TOP THREE THINGS THAT MADE YOUR CLIENT PROUD OF IT?

WHAT'S BEEN YOUR EASIEST PROJECT SO FAR IN TERMS OF GETTING IT APPROVED?

WHY DO YOU THINK IT WENT SO SMOOTHLY?

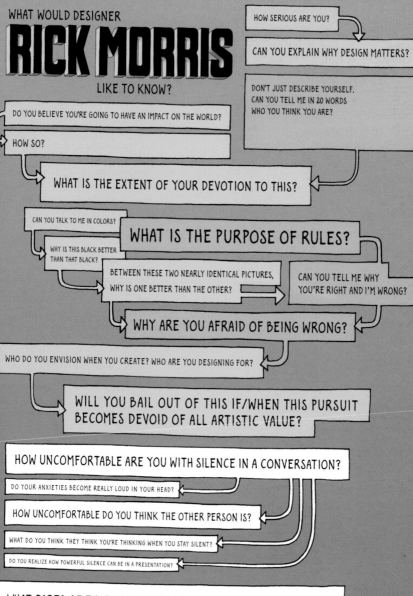

WHAT WOULD DESIGNER

RICK MORRIS

LIKE TO KNOW?

HOW SERIOUS ARE YOU?

CAN YOU EXPLAIN WHY DESIGN MATTERS?

DON'T JUST DESCRIBE YOURSELF. CAN YOU TELL ME IN 20 WORDS WHO YOU THINK YOU ARE?

DO YOU BELIEVE YOU'RE GOING TO HAVE AN IMPACT ON THE WORLD?

HOW SO?

WHAT IS THE EXTENT OF YOUR DEVOTION TO THIS?

CAN YOU TALK TO ME IN COLORS?

WHAT IS THE PURPOSE OF RULES?

WHY IS THIS BLACK BETTER THAN THAT BLACK?

BETWEEN THESE TWO NEARLY IDENTICAL PICTURES, WHY IS ONE BETTER THAN THE OTHER?

CAN YOU TELL ME WHY YOU'RE RIGHT AND I'M WRONG?

WHY ARE YOU AFRAID OF BEING WRONG?

WHO DO YOU ENVISION WHEN YOU CREATE? WHO ARE YOU DESIGNING FOR?

WILL YOU BAIL OUT OF THIS IF/WHEN THIS PURSUIT BECOMES DEVOID OF ALL ARTISTIC VALUE?

HOW UNCOMFORTABLE ARE YOU WITH SILENCE IN A CONVERSATION?

DO YOUR ANXIETIES BECOME REALLY LOUD IN YOUR HEAD?

HOW UNCOMFORTABLE DO YOU THINK THE OTHER PERSON IS?

WHAT DO YOU THINK THEY THINK YOU'RE THINKING WHEN YOU STAY SILENT?

DO YOU REALIZE HOW POWERFUL SILENCE CAN BE IN A PRESENTATION?

WHAT PARTS OF THAT CAN BECOME UNIVERSAL FOR YOUR WORK?

ARE YOU SELLING OUT?

FIRST OF ALL, WHAT DO YOU THINK ACTUALLY CONSTITUTES "SELLING OUT"?

IS IT DOING HALF-ASSED WORK FOR GREAT CLIENTS?

WHICH IS WORSE?

IS IT DOING GREAT WORK FOR HALF-ASSED CLIENTS?

IS IT DOING ANY WORK AT ALL FOR CLIENTS YOU WOULD PUT IN LIFE'S "EVIL" COLUMN IF IT WEREN'T FOR THEIR TASTY, TASTY PAYCHECK?

IS IT REHASHING OLD IDEAS OVER AND OVER JUST BECAUSE IT'S EASY?

OR IS THAT ACTUALLY PART OF ACHIEVING MASTERY?

OR REFINING YOUR ARTISTIC VOICE?

DO YOU THINK IT'S SELLING OUT TO DO A HIGH-PAYING JOB FOR A COMPANY YOU DON'T OTHERWISE SUPPORT IF THEIR MONEY CAN FUND A SELF-GENERATED PROJECT THAT YOU OTHERWISE COULDN'T AFFORD?

HOW DO YOU FEEL ABOUT THE ARGUMENT "IF I DON'T DO IT, SOMEBODY ELSE WILL?"

WHICH TEN PEOPLE OR COMPANIES WOULD YOU NEVER WORK FOR?

WHY?

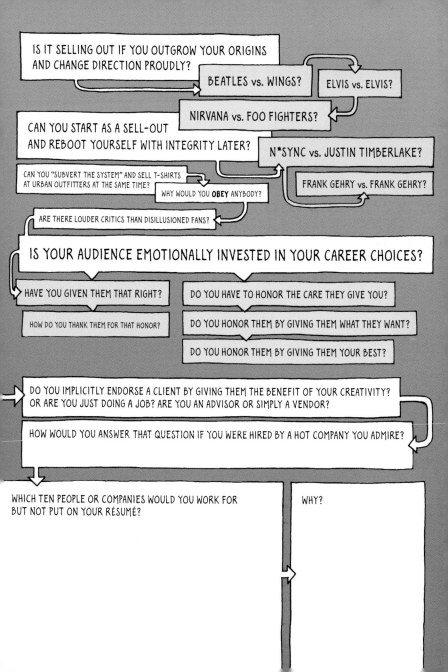

HOW DO YOU FIND THE KIND OF WORK YOU WANT TO DO?

JUST TO RECAP, WHAT ARE THE THREE THINGS ANY JOB OR ASSIGNMENT MUST OFFER TO MAKE IT WORTHWHILE FOR YOU?

AND WHAT ARE THE THREE THINGS THAT MAKE IT SOMETHING YOU KNOW YOU'LL END UP HATING OR RESENTING?

HOW CAN YOU GET BETTER AT RECOGNIZING THE FORMER, AND REMINDING YOURSELF OF THE LATTER?

WHAT ARE THE FIVE EASIEST PLACES TO FIND PEOPLE LOOKING FOR SOMEBODY LIKE YOU?

WHAT ARE THE FIVE EASIEST PLACES TO INTRODUCE YOURSELF TO PEOPLE WHO DON'T EVEN KNOW THEY NEED YOUR HELP YET?

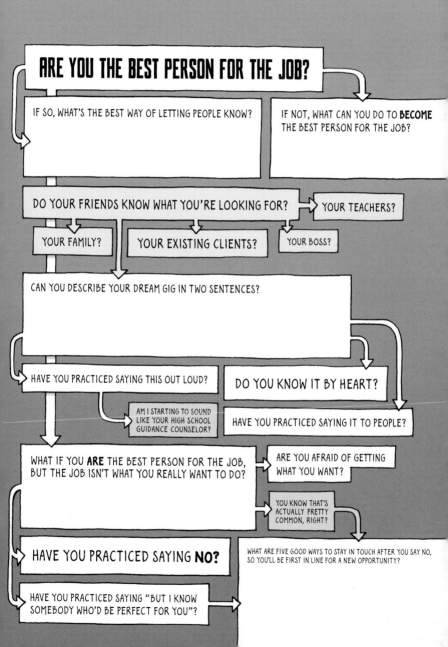

IS IT YOUR DUTY TO WALK THE WALK AFTER YOU'VE TALKED THE TALK?

WHAT IF THINGS CHANGE IN A WAY YOU COULDN'T FORESEE?

IS IT BETTER TO KEEP YOUR WORD AND SOLDIER ON NO MATTER WHAT?

OR TO REACT HONORABLY TO A CHANGED SITUATION?

IS THAT ANSWER THE SAME IN EVERY CIRCUMSTANCE?

WHEN SHOULD YOU BE A HYPOCRITE?

CAN YOU THINK OF A SITUATION WHEN YOU'D ABANDON A PROJECT OR GO BACK ON YOUR WORD?

CAN YOU THINK OF FIVE MORE SITUATIONS?

HOW LONG DID THAT TAKE YOU?

ARE YOU SURPRISED BY THAT?

WHAT'S THE DIFFERENCE BETWEEN BEING WEAK-WILLED AND CHANGING YOUR MIND?

IS THERE A STATUTE OF LIMITATIONS ON YOUR PAST DECISIONS?

WHAT'S THE DIFFERENCE BETWEEN INTEGRITY AND INFLEXIBILITY?

DO YOU JUDGE OTHERS BY THE SAME STANDARDS YOU APPLY TO YOURSELF?

ARE YOU HARMING YOURSELF BY STAYING TRUE TO PROMISES YOU MADE AT A VERY DIFFERENT TIME?

TO OTHERS?

TO YOURSELF?

WOULD THEY FORGIVE YOU IF YOU LET GO OF THE PARTICULARS OF A PROMISE IF YOU HONORED THE UNDERLYING SPIRIT?

WOULD YOU FORGIVE YOURSELF?

OR IS MORAL RELATIVISM JUST TOO CORROSIVE FOR THE SOUL?

HOW DO YOU DETERMINE WHAT WILL DO MORE DAMAGE TO ALL INVOLVED — STAYING IN A PAINFUL SITUATION UNTIL THE BITTER END, OR WALKING AWAY?

HAVE YOU ASKED HOW **THEY** FEEL?

IS A PROFESSIONAL COMMITMENT A SACRED OATH?

WHEN DO YOU KNOW THAT IT'S TIME TO WALK AWAY FROM A SITUATION?

CAN YOU CLEARLY ARTICULATE WHAT'S NOT AS IT SHOULD BE?

IS THE REASON EXTERNAL?

IS IT TEMPORARY?

IS IT A PROBLEM YOU CAN FIX BY ADDRESSING IT HEAD ON?

IS IT INHERENT TO THE SITUATION?

IS IT A PERSONALITY CONFLICT?

ARE YOU MORE HELPFUL TO THE PEOPLE YOU SET OUT TO HELP BY **STAYING** OR BY **LEAVING?**

WOULD THEY BE SAD TO SEE YOU GO?

HOW DO YOU HANDLE GUILT?

HAVE YOU EVER USED GUILT AS A WEAPON?

WOULD YOUR LEAVING CRIPPLE THE PROJECT?

HAS ANYONE EVER USED GUILT AS A WEAPON AGAINST YOU?

WOULD LEAVING HURT YOUR CAREER?

HOW EASILY WOULD YOU BE REPLACED?

WOULD LEAVING MAKE YOU HAPPY?

IF YOU **HAD** TO LEAVE, HOW COULD YOU DO IT WITH THE LEAST POSSIBLE DAMAGE TO THE WORK, TO YOUR PARTNERS, OR TO YOURSELF?

WHAT WOULD DESIGNER

JAKOB TROLLBÄCK

LIKE TO KNOW?

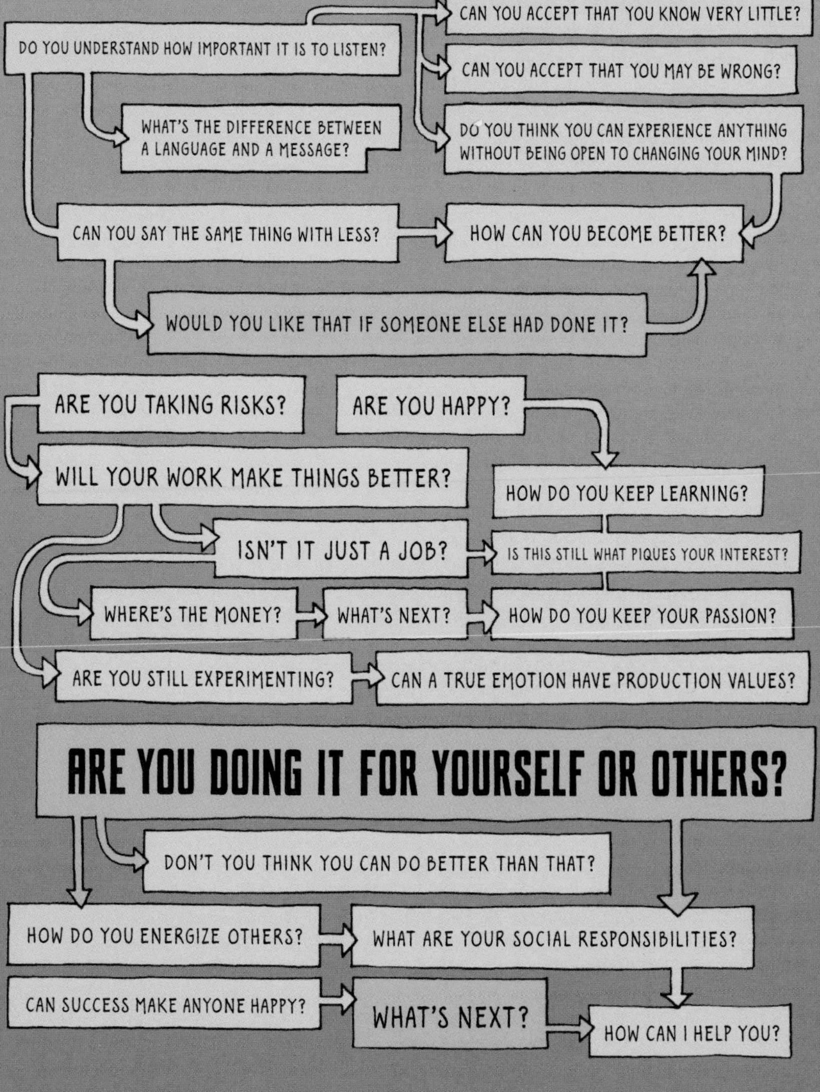

WHAT WOULD PHOTOGRAPHER JILL GREENBERG LIKE TO KNOW?

What questions do you wish somebody had asked you when you were a student?

IS THAT CHIP ON YOUR SHOULDER BIG ENOUGH TO MOTIVATE YOUR SENSE OF COMPETITION?

DO HONEST WORK FOR YOURSELF **OR** WORK FOR MULTINATIONAL CORPORATIONS. IT REALLY CAN'T BE BOTH. WHICH ONE DO YOU CHOOSE?

ARE YOU WILLING TO PRETEND YOU HAVE NO EGO TO YOUR CLIENTS?

WHY HAVEN'T YOU READ "HOW TO WIN FRIENDS AND INFLUENCE PEOPLE" BY DALE CARNEGIE?

ARE YOU WILLING TO SCHMOOZE AND SELL YOURSELF UNTIL YOU RETIRE?

ARE YOU WILLING TO WORK NIGHTS AND WEEKENDS TO ACCOMPLISH YOUR GOALS, PUTTING YOUR CAREER ABOVE EVERYTHING?

DO YOU REALIZE THAT SOME OF THE THEMES AND IDEAS WHICH INTEREST YOU NOW WILL ALWAYS INFORM YOUR WORK?

DO YOU REALLY THINK ONLY CIGARETTE AND FUR ADVERTISING IS EVIL? WHAT ABOUT COMPANIES THAT USE UNDERAGE LABOR AND TOXIC CHEMICALS? WHY DRAW THE LINE AT ALL?

WHAT DO YOU HAVE TO SAY?

WHAT ARE YOU GOING TO DO ABOUT THE RACE TO THE BOTTOM IN CREATIVE FEES AND IMAGE RIGHTS?

What questions do you wish somebody had asked you a year ago?

ARE YOU EXPLORING TOO MANY NEW DIRECTIONS?

ARE YOU STILL HAVING FUN?

WHY DID YOU CHOOSE TO IGNORE WHAT YOU LEARNED IN "HOW TO WIN FRIENDS AND INFLUENCE PEOPLE"?

AREN'T YOU FRUSTRATED WITH THE LACK OF COMMUNITY THAT PHOTOGRAPHERS HAVE?

What questions would only your closest friends know to ask you?

WHY DO YOU STILL (HAVE TO) WORK SO HARD?

DO YOU AGREE WITH THE PHRASE "IMITATION IS THE HIGHEST FORM OF FLATTERY"?

WHAT ARE YOU GOING TO DO NEXT?

DO YOU HAVE TO CHOOSE COMMERCIAL VERSUS FINE ART CAREERS?

ARE MAGAZINES STILL GOING TO EXPECT YOU TO FLY COACH WHEN YOU ARE 55? 65?

IS THE COMMERCIAL WORK INTERFERING WITH YOUR LEGITIMACY AS A FINE ARTIST?

ARE WORK MORALS AND PERSONAL MORALS THE SAME? IS LYING OK IN BUSINESS?

HOW DOES IT MAKE YOU FEEL WHEN YOUR CLIENTS LIE TO YOU?

DO YOU FEEL MISUNDERSTOOD?

ARE YOU GOING TO REGRET NOT SPENDING ENOUGH TIME WITH YOUR CHILDREN?

DO YOU WANT TO HAVE A STABLE LIFE?

DO YOU WANT TO HAVE AN INTERESTING LIFE?

TO WHAT DEGREE ARE YOU WILLING AND ABLE TO TRADE ONE FOR THE OTHER?

ARE YOU LEGALLY AND MORALLY RESPONSIBLE FOR THE HEALTH AND WELL-BEING OF OTHERS?

DO YOU WANT TO BE A FORCE FOR GOOD IN THE WORLD?

OR IS "DO NO HARM" GOOD ENOUGH?

DO YOU SEE YOURSELF AS AN ADVOCATE?

DO YOU ENJOY MAKING THINGS HAPPEN?

OR DO YOU GET MORE PLEASURE FROM BEING SUPPORTIVE OF THE PEOPLE AROUND YOU?

WHAT IS YOUR PURPOSE?

AT AGE 120, AS YOUR BRAIN IS UPLOADED INTO THE CENTRAL INTELLIGENCE ARRAY, WHAT WILL BE YOUR TEN PROUDEST ACHIEVEMENTS OR FONDEST MEMORIES?

HOW MANY OF THOSE THINGS ARE ALREADY IN YOUR PAST TODAY?

WHAT WILL YOU DO TODAY TO GET CLOSER TO MAKING THE REST OF THEM REAL?

How do you define "Nirvana"?

(or aligns with/contradicts what you preach)

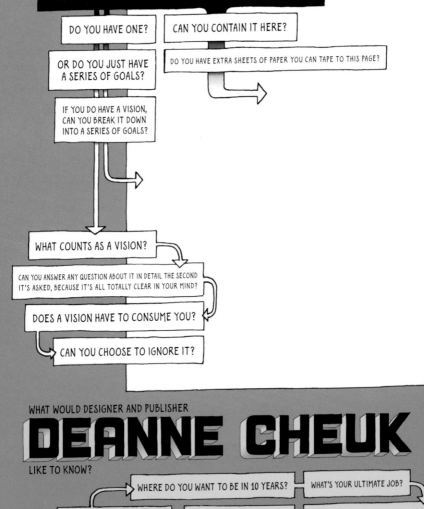

WHAT IS YOUR VISION?

DO YOU HAVE ONE?

CAN YOU CONTAIN IT HERE?

OR DO YOU JUST HAVE A SERIES OF GOALS?

DO YOU HAVE EXTRA SHEETS OF PAPER YOU CAN TAPE TO THIS PAGE?

IF YOU DO HAVE A VISION, CAN YOU BREAK IT DOWN INTO A SERIES OF GOALS?

WHAT COUNTS AS A VISION?

CAN YOU ANSWER ANY QUESTION ABOUT IT IN DETAIL THE SECOND IT'S ASKED, BECAUSE IT'S ALL TOTALLY CLEAR IN YOUR MIND?

DOES A VISION HAVE TO CONSUME YOU?

CAN YOU CHOOSE TO IGNORE IT?

WHAT WOULD DESIGNER AND PUBLISHER

DEANNE CHEUK

LIKE TO KNOW?

WHERE DO YOU WANT TO BE IN 10 YEARS?

WHAT'S YOUR ULTIMATE JOB?

WHERE DO YOU WANT TO WORK?

WHERE DO YOU WANT TO LIVE?

WHAT DO YOU ENJOY WORKING ON?

WHAT DO YOU WANT TO LEARN?

WHO DO YOU WANT TO LEARN FROM?

CAN YOU DREAM EVEN BIGGER?

WOULD YOU LIKE A DESIGNATED SPACE FOR YOUR INNER VISIONS?

WHAT DO YOU WANT TO GIVE?

HOW WILL YOU FIND YOUR VOICE?

YOUR **VOICE?** WHAT DOES THAT EVEN MEAN, FIND YOUR **VOICE?**

IS THAT SOMETHING YOU WORRY ABOUT WHILE YOU'RE AVOIDING YOUR WORK?

IS YOUR VOICE SOMETHING YOU CAN DECIDE ON?

OR IS IT SOMETHING YOU DISCOVER IN RETROSPECT, SOMETHING THAT BECOMES APPARENT WHEN YOU LOOK BACK AT ALL THE WORK YOU'VE ACCUMULATED OVER YEARS AND YEARS?

IS IT TOO SOON TO THINK ABOUT THAT?

LIKE CHARACTER?

OR THOSE 20 EXTRA POUNDS?

IS IT LIKE LOOKING AT YOUR FEET WHILE YOU'RE DANCING?

OR IS IT USEFUL TO SPEND A FEW MINUTES EVERY FEW YEARS THINKING ABOUT WHAT YOU WANT YOUR WORK TO SAY, AND WHAT YOU WANT IT TO SOUND OR LOOK OR FEEL LIKE WHEN PEOPLE ENCOUNTER IT?

IF YOU HAD TO DESCRIBE YOUR WORK AS YOU WOULD DESCRIBE A PERSON, WHAT WOULD IT LOOK LIKE?

HOW OLD WOULD IT BE?

WHAT WOULD IT WEAR?

WHO WOULD IT VOTE FOR?

WHO WOULD IT SOUND LIKE?

WHAT MUSIC WOULD IT LISTEN TO?

WHAT, IF ANYTHING, WOULD YOU CHANGE ABOUT THAT?

IS THE BACK OF YOUR HEAD THE BEST PLACE FOR THIS INFORMATION?

IS IT JUST A MATTER OF TIME?

IS THERE ANY ACTION YOU CAN TAKE?

WHAT WOULD ILLUSTRATOR

MARTHA RICH

LIKE TO KNOW?

WHAT MAKES YOU THINK YOU CAN DO THIS?

WHAT HAVE YOU GOT TO LOSE?

ARE YOU SURE YOU WANT THAT CREDIT CARD?

WHY ARE YOU PUTTING THAT IN YOUR PORTFOLIO?

ARE YOU WILLING TO WORK LONG AND HARD?

DO YOU KNOW HOW TO HANDLE MONEY?

WHO ARE YOU?

ARE YOU SURE A PUPPET IS THE BEST METAPHOR YOU CAN COME UP WITH?

CAN YOU HANDLE REJECTION AND FAILURE?

WHAT IS SO WRONG WITH BEING COMFORTABLE?

WHAT IS THE POINT?

WHY ARE YOU GOING BACK TO SCHOOL AT THIS AGE?

DO YOU REALIZE GRADUATE SCHOOL IS EXPENSIVE?

DO YOU REMEMBER THAT THE EAST COAST IS COLD IN THE WINTER?

DO YOU HAVE ENOUGH SOCKS?

WHO ARE YOU?

IS THIS REALLY SOMETHING YOU WANT TO DO OR ARE YOU AVOIDING DEALING WITH LIFE?

IS IT WORTH IT?

WHY DO YOU CARE SO MUCH WHAT OTHER PEOPLE THINK?

WOULD YOU LIKE TO GO ON A DATE?

DO YOU WANT TO GO ON A ROAD TRIP AND EXPLORE?

WOULD YOU LIKE TO COME OVER FOR A GLASS OF WINE?

ARE YOU CENSORING YOURSELF?

CAN YOU TELL THEM NO?

CAN I COOK YOU DINNER?

WHAT THE HELL WERE YOU THINKING?

ARE YOU SURE YOU WANT TO TAKE THAT ON?

ARE YOU CATASTROPHIZING?

DO YOU REALLY NEED THAT DONUT?

WHY DO YOU KEEP OBSESSING OVER BEING OLD?

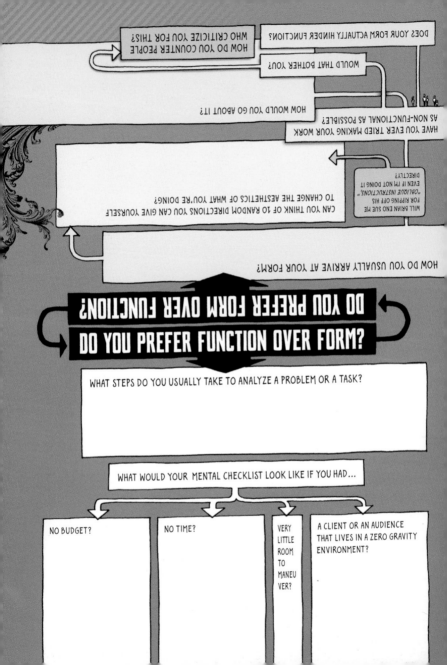

DO YOU PREFER FUNCTION OVER FORM?

WHAT STEPS DO YOU USUALLY TAKE TO ANALYZE A PROBLEM OR A TASK?

WHAT WOULD YOUR MENTAL CHECKLIST LOOK LIKE IF YOU HAD...

NO BUDGET?

NO TIME?

VERY LITTLE ROOM TO MANEUVER?

A CLIENT OR AN AUDIENCE THAT LIVES IN A ZERO GRAVITY ENVIRONMENT?

DO YOU PREFER FORM OVER FUNCTION?

HOW DO YOU USUALLY ARRIVE AT YOUR FORM?

CAN YOU THINK OF 10 RANDOM DIRECTIONS YOU CAN GIVE YOURSELF TO CHANGE THE AESTHETICS OF WHAT YOU'RE DOING?

WILL BRIAN ENO SUE ME FOR RIPPING OFF HIS "OBLIQUE INSTRUCTIONS," EVEN IF I'M NOT DOING IT DIRECTLY?

HAVE YOU EVER TRIED MAKING YOUR WORK AS NON-FUNCTIONAL AS POSSIBLE?

HOW WOULD YOU GO ABOUT IT?

WOULD THAT BOTHER YOU?

DOES YOUR FORM ACTUALLY HINDER FUNCTION?

HOW DO YOU COUNTER PEOPLE WHO CRITICIZE YOU FOR THIS?

WHAT WOULD COMPOSER

DAVID NORLAND

LIKE TO KNOW?

WHAT IF ALL YOUR ASSUMPTIONS TO DATE ABOUT YOUR PURPOSE HERE ARE WRONG?

WHAT IF THOSE WHO HAVE INFORMED YOUR WORLDVIEW (AND SELF-VIEW) ARE THEMSELVES MISINFORMED?

HOW OFTEN DOES FEAR MOTIVATE THE CHOICES YOU MAKE, ON ALL SCALES FROM MACRO TO NANO?

WHOSE VOICE RULES IN YOUR HEAD?

DOES IT VARY?

WHAT IS COURAGE?

DON'T YOU THINK YOUR LIFE MIGHT BENEFIT FROM A BIT OF IT?

HOW BIG A GAP IS THERE BETWEEN YOUR ARTISTIC IDEALS AND YOUR OWN PRACTICE?

WHO WILL CHANGE THAT IF YOU DON'T?

WHY HAVEN'T YOU GOT AN ASSISTANT YET?

WHO DO YOU HOPE WILL/FEAR WON'T FALL IN LOVE WITH YOU AS A RESULT OF YOUR ART?

WHY IS THAT SO IMPORTANT TO YOU?

WHY HAVEN'T YOU GOT RID OF THAT RECORDING CONSOLE?

DO YOU REALLY THINK POP IS NOW TRULY DEAD AS A CREATIVE FORM, AND SHOULDN'T YOU GIVE IT ONE MORE CHANCE?

WHEN WAS THE LAST TIME YOU WORKED "STREAM-OF-CONSCIOUSNESS"?

WHY ARE YOU HOLDING ON TO VINTAGE SYNTHS YOU NEVER USE?

DON'T YOU THINK YOU SHOULD GET SOME SLEEP?

WHAT PATTERNS ARE YOU CLINGING TO?

WHY?

WHY DOES IT TAKE YOU SO LONG TO LEARN THE SIMPLE TRUTH THAT CHANGE TENDS TO BE INSPIRING: DON'T FEAR IT, SEEK IT OUT?

ARE YOU WILLING TO CHANGE?

WHAT ARE YOU GOING AS NEXT HALLOWEEN?

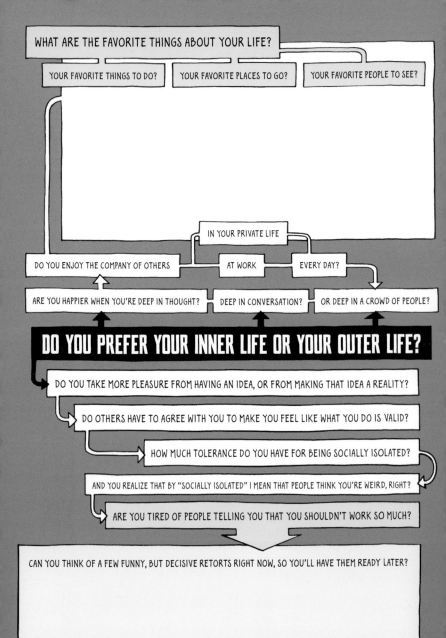

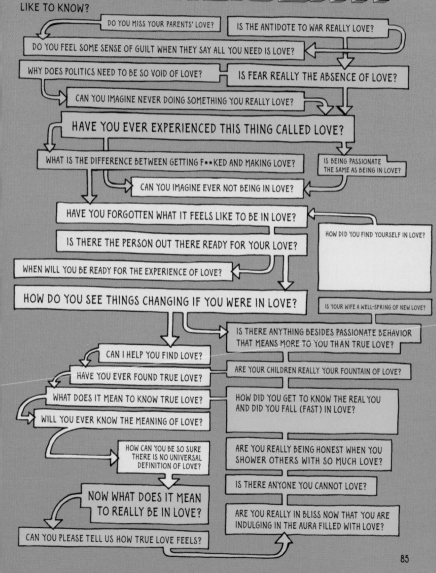

85

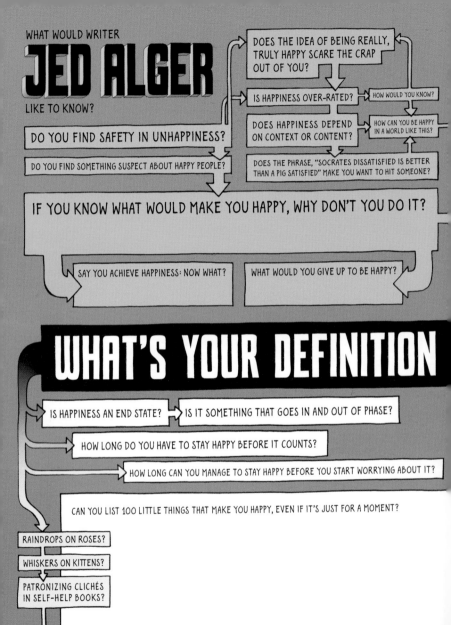

WHAT WOULD WRITER

JED ALGER

LIKE TO KNOW?

DOES THE IDEA OF BEING REALLY, TRULY HAPPY SCARE THE CRAP OUT OF YOU?

IS HAPPINESS OVER-RATED?

HOW WOULD YOU KNOW?

DOES HAPPINESS DEPEND ON CONTEXT OR CONTENT?

HOW CAN YOU BE HAPPY IN A WORLD LIKE THIS?

DO YOU FIND SAFETY IN UNHAPPINESS?

DO YOU FIND SOMETHING SUSPECT ABOUT HAPPY PEOPLE?

DOES THE PHRASE, "SOCRATES DISSATISFIED IS BETTER THAN A PIG SATISFIED" MAKE YOU WANT TO HIT SOMEONE?

IF YOU KNOW WHAT WOULD MAKE YOU HAPPY, WHY DON'T YOU DO IT?

SAY YOU ACHIEVE HAPPINESS: NOW WHAT?

WHAT WOULD YOU GIVE UP TO BE HAPPY?

WHAT'S YOUR DEFINITION

IS HAPPINESS AN END STATE?

IS IT SOMETHING THAT GOES IN AND OUT OF PHASE?

HOW LONG DO YOU HAVE TO STAY HAPPY BEFORE IT COUNTS?

HOW LONG CAN YOU MANAGE TO STAY HAPPY BEFORE YOU START WORRYING ABOUT IT?

CAN YOU LIST 100 LITTLE THINGS THAT MAKE YOU HAPPY, EVEN IF IT'S JUST FOR A MOMENT?

RAINDROPS ON ROSES?

WHISKERS ON KITTENS?

PATRONIZING CLICHÉS IN SELF-HELP BOOKS?

ARE YOU PREPARED FOR THE WORST?

ARE YOU PREPARED FOR THE PRETTY DAMN BAD?

OH SHIT! WHAT

WHAT WOULD YOU CONSIDER THE TEN WORST THINGS
THAT COULD HAPPEN IN YOUR WORK OR IN YOUR LIFE?

WHICH OF THOSE THINGS ARE UNDER YOUR CONTROL?

WHICH OF THEM WOULD THREATEN YOUR ABILITY TO MAKE A LIVING?

WHICH OF THEM WOULD THREATEN YOUR LIFE?

WHICH OF THEM WOULD HAVE A MAJOR EFFECT ON PEOPLE AROUND YOU?

CAN YOU HELP THEM?

FOR WHICH OF THOSE THINGS CAN YOU PREPARE?

DO YOU HAVE AN EMERGENCY FUND?

DO YOU HAVE A CURRENT RÉSUMÉ?

DO YOU CARRY THE RIGHT KIND OF INSURANCE?

DO YOU KEEP YOURSELF AND YOUR WORK VISIBLE?

IS PEACE OF MIND SOMETHING YOU CARE ABOUT?

OR DOES IT JUST SLOW YOU DOWN?

CAN YOU PREPARE FOR THE WORST AND MOVE ON?

OR WILL YOU OBSESS ABOUT IT?

CAN YOU DO IT AT THE SAME TIME WITH FRIENDS?

JUST HAPPENED?

ARE YOU AFRAID OF CALAMITY?

Are you afriad of feeling stupid?

WHAT HAVE YOU LEARNED THAT WILL HELP YOU NEXT TIME DISASTER STRIKES?

HAVE ANY OF THEM HAPPENED ALREADY?

DID THEY MAKE YOU STRONGER?

OR DID THEY JUST SUCK?

DO YOU LIVE IN AN EARTHQUAKE OR FLOOD ZONE?

HAVE YOU ASSEMBLED YOUR DISASTER KIT?

DO YOU HAVE ENOUGH WATER IN RESERVE?

DON'T YOU THINK SOME CHOCOLATE RESERVES WOULD OFFER AT LEAST A MOMENT'S SOLACE, EVEN DURING A MAJOR CATASTROPHE?

DO YOU BACK UP YOUR FILES?

IN TWO SEPARATE PLACES?

DID YOU KNOW THAT PEANUT BUTTER IS AN EXCELLENT EMERGENCY FOOD BECAUSE IT HAS A LONG SHELF LIFE AND IS VERY ENERGY-RICH?

HAVE YOU WRITTEN OUT A LIST OF YOUR MAJOR ACCOUNT IDs AND PASSWORDS?

WHAT ARE THE ODDS THAT YOU WON'T EAT ALL THOSE CHOCOLATE AND PEANUT BUTTER RATIONS RIGHT AWAY?

HAVE YOU TOLD SOMEBODY YOU TRUST WHERE TO FIND THAT LIST IN CASE YOU CAN'T GET TO IT?

HAVE YOU MADE A LIVING WILL?

HAVE YOU REGISTERED AS AN ORGAN DONOR?

WOULD YOU MAKE UP AN EXCUSE, LIKE "I COULD SWEAR THAT I FELT A QUAKE EARLIER, A 3.5 AT LEAST"?

HAVE YOU MADE A LAST WILL?

DO YOU THINK YOU'RE TOO YOUNG FOR ALL THIS STUFF?

DO YOU BELIEVE IN KNOCKING ON WOOD?

DO YOU BELIEVE IN LOOKING LEFT AND RIGHT BEFORE CROSSING THE STREET?

DO YOU BELIEVE IN THE EXISTENCE OF PEOPLE WHO TEXT WHILE DRIVING?

89

ARE TIMES TOUGH FOR EXTERNAL OR INTERNAL REASONS?

CAN YOU THINK OR ACT YOUR WAY OUT OF THIS?

OR DO YOU HAVE TO RIDE IT OUT?

HOW DO YOU GET THROUGH TOUGH TIMES?

CAN WE FOCUS ON THE IMMEDIATE ESSENTIALS?

WHAT FOODS MAKE YOU HAPPY?

WHAT TV SHOWS DISTRACT YOU?

WHAT MUSIC PERKS YOU UP?

DO YOU HAVE AN EMERGENCY SUPPLY OF ALL THIS STUFF?

DO YOU HAVE FRIENDS WHO'LL LISTEN TO YOU? → WHAT ARE THEIR PHONE NUMBERS?

DO YOU HAVE FRIENDS **YOU'LL** LISTEN TO? →

ON A SCALE OF 1 TO 10, HOW BAD IS THIS ONE?

1   2   3   4   5   6   7   8   9   10

IS THE WORST ALREADY OVER? → OR IS IT GOING TO GET WORSE BEFORE IT GETS BETTER?

WHAT WOULD BE THE MOST HELPFUL THING FOR YOU RIGHT NOW?

IS THERE ANY WAY FOR YOU TO MAKE THAT HAPPEN?

WILL YOU PLEASE ACCEPT MY GOOD WISHES THAT IT'LL ALL WORK OUT FOR YOU IN THE END?

WHAT WOULD PRODUCTION DESIGNER AND AUTHOR

DOUG CHIANG

LIKE TO KNOW?

CAN YOU DRAW ME SOMETHING I HAVEN'T SEEN BEFORE?

WHAT DO YOU THINK IS MORE IMPORTANT?
TALENT OR HARD WORK?

DO YOU THINK BEING AN ARTIST WILL MAKE YOU HAPPY?

HOW CAN YOU KNOW WHAT STEPS TO TAKE IF YOU DON'T KNOW WHERE YOU ARE GOING?

CAN YOU TELL ME WHAT YOU WANT?

CAN YOU TELL ME WHAT YOU DON'T WANT?

WHAT ARE YOU DOING TODAY TO ACHIEVE YOUR DREAMS?

CAN YOU TELL ME THREE THINGS TO DO THAT'LL GET YOU CLOSER TO WHAT YOU WANT?

WHAT IS PREVENTING YOU FROM FOLLOWING YOUR BLISS?

IS PASSION ALL YOU'VE GOT?   IS TALENT OVERRATED?

WHY CAN'T YOU SLEEP AT 4 AM?   WHAT ARE YOU HIDING BEHIND BOLDNESS?

CAN YOU LET GO OF YOUR DREAMS AND STILL BE HAPPY?

WHY DO YOU DRIVE YOURSELF CRAZY WITH DETAILS THAT NOBODY CARES ABOUT?   CAN YOU STOP WORRYING ABOUT BEING OBSOLETE?

HOW MUCH SUCCESS IS SUCCESS?   WHEN IS "GOOD ENOUGH" ENOUGH?

ARE YOU BLINDED BY YOUR DREAMS?

WHAT IS YOUR WORST CASE SCENARIO?

WHAT ARE THE ODDS OF THAT?

HAVE YOU SEEN IT HAPPEN TO ANYBODY YOU KNOW?

HOW DID THEY HANDLE IT?

WHAT IS THE COST OF TAKING PRECAUTIONS AGAINST IT?

WHAT CAN YOU LEARN FROM THEIR EXPERIENCE?

HAVE YOU FACTORED IN YOUR COST IN TIME, FEAR, LOST OPPORTUNITIES? WHAT ABOUT LOST JOY?

IS YOUR WORST CASE SCENARIO SO DEVASTATING THAT YOU HAVE TO PROTECT YOURSELF EVEN IF THE COST SEEMS UNREASONABLE, AND THE ODDS ARE OVERWHELMINGLY IN YOUR FAVOR?

WHAT CAN YOU DO TO MINIMIZE THE PSYCHIC DRAIN OF HAVING TO DEAL WITH THESE SAFETY MEASURES?

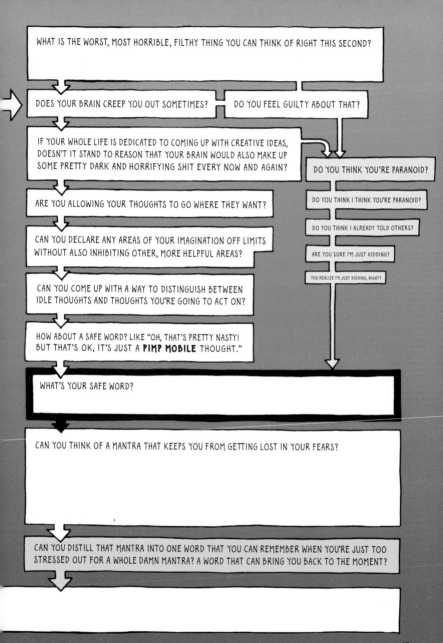

WHAT IS THE WORST, MOST HORRIBLE, FILTHY THING YOU CAN THINK OF RIGHT THIS SECOND?

DOES YOUR BRAIN CREEP YOU OUT SOMETIMES?

DO YOU FEEL GUILTY ABOUT THAT?

IF YOUR WHOLE LIFE IS DEDICATED TO COMING UP WITH CREATIVE IDEAS, DOESN'T IT STAND TO REASON THAT YOUR BRAIN WOULD ALSO MAKE UP SOME PRETTY DARK AND HORRIFYING SHIT EVERY NOW AND AGAIN?

DO YOU THINK YOU'RE PARANOID?

ARE YOU ALLOWING YOUR THOUGHTS TO GO WHERE THEY WANT?

DO YOU THINK I THINK YOU'RE PARANOID?

CAN YOU DECLARE ANY AREAS OF YOUR IMAGINATION OFF LIMITS WITHOUT ALSO INHIBITING OTHER, MORE HELPFUL AREAS?

DO YOU THINK I ALREADY TOLD OTHERS?

CAN YOU COME UP WITH A WAY TO DISTINGUISH BETWEEN IDLE THOUGHTS AND THOUGHTS YOU'RE GOING TO ACT ON?

ARE YOU SURE I'M JUST KIDDING?

YOU REALIZE I'M JUST KIDDING, RIGHT?

HOW ABOUT A SAFE WORD? LIKE "OH, THAT'S PRETTY NASTY! BUT THAT'S OK, IT'S JUST A **PIMP MOBILE** THOUGHT."

WHAT'S YOUR SAFE WORD?

CAN YOU THINK OF A MANTRA THAT KEEPS YOU FROM GETTING LOST IN YOUR FEARS?

CAN YOU DISTILL THAT MANTRA INTO ONE WORD THAT YOU CAN REMEMBER WHEN YOU'RE JUST TOO STRESSED OUT FOR A WHOLE DAMN MANTRA? A WORD THAT CAN BRING YOU BACK TO THE MOMENT?

WHAT IS YOUR BEST CASE SCENARIO?

IS THAT OPTIMISTIC ENOUGH?

HAVE YOU BECOME **TOO REALISTIC** AND **TOO SERIOUS** TO DREAM BIG?

WHAT IF YOUR BEST CASE SCENARIO IS JUST THE BEGINNING?

WHAT IF YOU MULTIPLY "BEST CASE SCENARIO" TIMES "WILDEST DREAM"?

WHY SHOULDN'T THAT HAPPEN FOR YOU?

OR AN EVEN MORE FUN VERSION OF IT?

ARE YOU AS PREPARED FOR SUCCESS

IF A SUDDENLY SUCCESSFUL SITE CAN CRASH FROM TOO MANY HITS, WHAT WOULD HAPPEN TO YOUR BRAIN?

CAN YOU BUILD UP MORE MENTAL BANDWIDTH?

WHAT WOULD **THE ELECTRIC COMPANY**™ EXECUTIVE PRODUCER

KAREN FOWLER

LIKE TO KNOW?

WHERE ARE YOU THE MOST PLAYFUL, SILLIEST, CREATIVE, BIGGEST YOU?

IF YOU REACH FOR THE STARS AND MAKE IT TO THE TOPS OF THE TREES, HAVE YOU FAILED?

OR ARE YOU AN ASTRONAUT WHO ALSO SCALES HUGE TREES?

THE SUFIS SAY "FALL DOWN 7 TIMES, GET UP 8." DO YOU HAVE ENOUGH BANDAGES?

HOW DO YOU TELL YOUR STORY?

IS IT WEIRD TO SMILE AT STRANGERS?

IS KINDNESS OPTIONAL?

WHAT'S THE SOUNDTRACK?

CAN BITING YOUR TONGUE BE THE PAIN THAT BRINGS THE GAIN?

DOES IT MAKE YOU GIGGLE?

WHAT WERE YOU MOST AFRAID OF AS A KID?

DOES IT INSPIRE YOU?

IF NOT, TRY WALKING AROUND IT AND RECAST YOURSELF AS AN INVETERATE INVENTOR, A SOULFUL SIREN OR A MONKEY. DOES THAT HELP?

WHAT ARE YOU MOST AFRAID OF TODAY?

WHY KEEP DOING WHAT YOU'RE DOING?

WHAT IF THAT FEAR IS JUST LIKE THE FEROCIOUS EVIL ALLIGATOR THAT USED TO HIDE UNDER YOUR BED (OR WAS THAT MINE?!) WHEN YOU WERE SEVEN YEARS OLD AND THEN YOU GREW UP AND DISCOVERED ... IT'S NOT THERE !?

JOY? MONEY? PRESTIGE?

LOVE? A HOT SHOWER?

WHERE WILL YOU PUT YOUR AWARDS? THE FRIDGE? THE BATHROOM? THE TROPHY SHELF?

BECAUSE YOU CAN'T HELP YOURSELF?

WHAT ARE THE SIX WORDS YOU WANT IMPRINTED ON THE HEARTS OF THOSE YOU LOVE?

AS YOU ARE FOR FAILURE?

WHAT DO YOU REALLY WANT TO DO?

WHAT ARE YOU WAITING FOR?

IF NOT YOU, THEN WHO?

YOU CAN TELL ME ... I PROMISE TO KEEP IT A SECRET UNTIL YOU'RE READY... ARE YOU READY NOW?

GOOD GAME, EH?

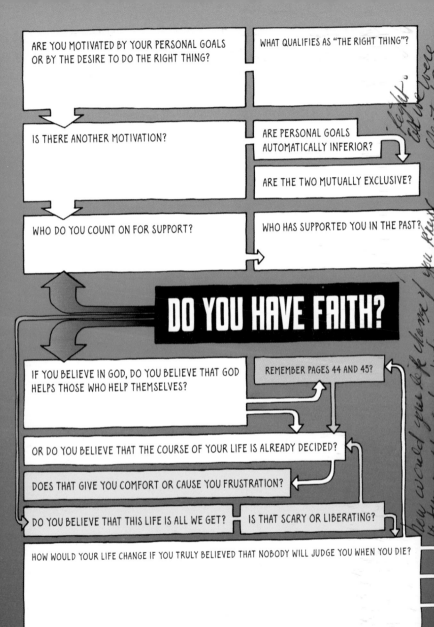

ARE YOU MOTIVATED BY YOUR PERSONAL GOALS OR BY THE DESIRE TO DO THE RIGHT THING?

WHAT QUALIFIES AS "THE RIGHT THING"?

IS THERE ANOTHER MOTIVATION?

ARE PERSONAL GOALS AUTOMATICALLY INFERIOR?

ARE THE TWO MUTUALLY EXCLUSIVE?

WHO DO YOU COUNT ON FOR SUPPORT?

WHO HAS SUPPORTED YOU IN THE PAST?

DO YOU HAVE FAITH?

IF YOU BELIEVE IN GOD, DO YOU BELIEVE THAT GOD HELPS THOSE WHO HELP THEMSELVES?

REMEMBER PAGES 44 AND 45?

OR DO YOU BELIEVE THAT THE COURSE OF YOUR LIFE IS ALREADY DECIDED?

DOES THAT GIVE YOU COMFORT OR CAUSE YOU FRUSTRATION?

DO YOU BELIEVE THAT THIS LIFE IS ALL WE GET?

IS THAT SCARY OR LIBERATING?

HOW WOULD YOUR LIFE CHANGE IF YOU TRULY BELIEVED THAT NOBODY WILL JUDGE YOU WHEN YOU DIE?

HOW WOULD YOU CHANGE THE WAY YOU LIVE YOUR LIFE AND DO YOUR WORK IF THE ONLY TWO RULES WERE "OBEY THE LAWS OF THE LAND" AND "TREAT OTHERS AS YOU WOULD WANT THEM TO TREAT YOU"?

USSR? Nazi Ger.? N. Korea?

What about those who want + try to deceive/use them?

WHAT WOULD YOU DO **TODAY** IF YOU KNEW THAT THOSE WERE THE ONLY TWO RULES?

DO YOU HAVE A PLAN?

WHAT OTHER RULES HAVE YOU SET FOR YOURSELF?

If the bottles know how to manipulate my loopholes?

NOW THAT YOU'VE WRITTEN THEM OUT, IS IT EASIER TO QUESTION THOSE RULES?

AND WILL THE RULES THAT STAND UP TO YOUR QUESTIONS BECOME EASIER TO FOLLOW AS YOU GO ON?

DO YOU THINK I'M OVERSTEPPING MY BOUNDS BY ASKING YOU THESE THINGS?

DO YOU BELIEVE THAT I MEAN WELL?

WOULD YOU BECOME AN EGOMANIAC DEVOID OF MORALS?

WOULD YOU FEEL ALONE?

WOULD YOU FEEL CURED?

WOULD YOU FEEL MORE CONNECTED TO YOUR FELLOW HUMANS, AND BECOME MORE COMPASSIONATE?

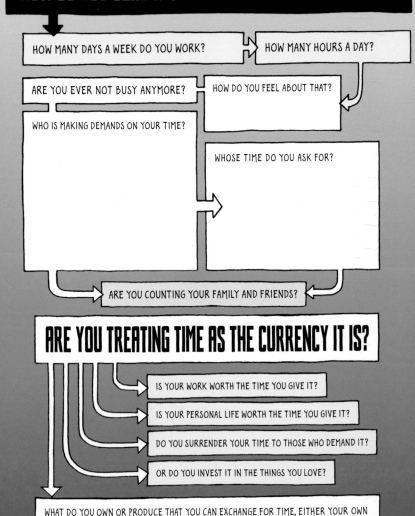

HOW DO YOU DEAL WITH LIMITS ON YOUR BANDWIDTH?

HOW MANY DAYS A WEEK DO YOU WORK?

HOW MANY HOURS A DAY?

ARE YOU EVER NOT BUSY ANYMORE?

HOW DO YOU FEEL ABOUT THAT?

WHO IS MAKING DEMANDS ON YOUR TIME?

WHOSE TIME DO YOU ASK FOR?

ARE YOU COUNTING YOUR FAMILY AND FRIENDS?

ARE YOU TREATING TIME AS THE CURRENCY IT IS?

IS YOUR WORK WORTH THE TIME YOU GIVE IT?

IS YOUR PERSONAL LIFE WORTH THE TIME YOU GIVE IT?

DO YOU SURRENDER YOUR TIME TO THOSE WHO DEMAND IT?

OR DO YOU INVEST IT IN THE THINGS YOU LOVE?

WHAT DO YOU OWN OR PRODUCE THAT YOU CAN EXCHANGE FOR TIME, EITHER YOUR OWN OR THAT OF OTHERS?

WHAT ARE THE FIVE EASIEST WAYS TO FREE UP EXISTING BANDWIDTH IN YOUR LIFE?

HOW CAN YOU EXPAND YOUR PERSONAL BANDWIDTH?

WHAT WOULD GRAPHIC DESIGNER

JAN WILKER

LIKE TO KNOW?

HAVE YOU BEEN GENEROUSLY GIVING ADVICE TO YOUR PEERS?

DO YOU SEE GIVING ADVICE TO YOUR PEERS AS WEAKENING YOUR OWN POSITION?

HAVE YOU RECEIVED GENEROUS ADVICE FROM YOUR PEERS?

ARE YOU A "CONTROL FREAK," WANTING TO DO EVERYTHING BY YOURSELF?

DO YOU GO TO A DOCTOR WHEN YOU'RE HURT OR DO YOU DIY VIA WEBMD.COM?

ARE YOU READY TO GIVE UP SOME RESPONSIBILITY (OR CONTROL) IN RETURN FOR LESS STRESS?

ARE YOU READY TO HAVE LESS STRESS IN RETURN FOR SHARED AUTHORSHIP?

DO YOU SEE YOURSELF AS A TRUSTED SPECIALIST THAT SHOULD BE SOUGHT OUT FOR PROFESSIONAL HELP?

COULD A THERAPIST HELP YOU BECOME A BETTER DESIGNER AND/OR A BETTER BUSINESSMAN?

WHAT DOES YOUR PERSONALITY HAVE TO DO WITH YOUR PROFESSION?

DOES "DESIGN" FEEL LIKE A HOBBY OR A PROFESSION TO YOU?

DO YOU TRY TO SHOW YOUR CLIENT THAT DESIGN IS INDEED A PROFESSION AND NOT A HOBBY?

DO YOU HAVE A SET PRICE LIST FOR YOUR SERVICES OR ARE YOU SETTING FEES ON A CASE-BY-CASE BASIS? WHY DO YOU THINK THAT IS?

ARE YOU PROUD TO BE A DESIGNER?

DO YOU RECEIVE THE RESPECT YOU THINK YOU DESERVE?

99

HOW DO YOU HANDLE TOO MUCH SUCCESS?

WHAT WOULD HAPPEN IF YOU ACTUALLY ACHIEVED EVERYTHING YOU WORKED FOR?

WOULD YOU STILL WANT IT IF IT WAS GRANTED TO YOU, INSTEAD OF EARNING IT YOURSELF?

WHAT IF YOU HAD EARNED EVERY BIT OF IT?

WHAT IF YOU GOT **WAY MORE** THAN THAT?

ARE YOU MORE INTERESTED IN THE GETTING OR THE HAVING?

REMEMBER WHAT SPOCK TOLD STON?

WOULD YOU KNOW WHEN TO SAY "ENOUGH"?

WHAT WOULD YOU DO TO KEEP WHAT YOU WORKED SO HARD FOR?

WHAT IF SAYING "ENOUGH" MEANT THAT PEOPLE THAT WORK FOR YOU LOSE THEIR JOB?

HOW FAR WOULD YOU CHANGE YOUR IDEAS?

WHAT IF IT MEANT YOUR KIDS COULDN'T GO TO THE BEST POSSIBLE SCHOOL?

HOW MUCH WOULD YOU CENSOR YOURSELF?

WHAT WOULD BRAND GURU AND AIGA PRESIDENT

DEBBIE MILLMAN

LIKE TO KNOW?

WHAT IS YOUR DEFINITION OF SUCCESS?

DO YOU THINK THERE IS A DIFFERENCE BETWEEN ACHIEVEMENT AND SUCCESS, AND IF SO, WHAT IS IT?

AFTER ACCOMPLISHING A GOAL, DO YOU FEEL A SENSE OF CONTENTMENT OR PRIDE, AND IF SO, **HOW LONG DOES IT LAST?**

HOW MUCH FAILURE CAN YOU TOLERATE?

IF AT FIRST YOU DON'T SUCCEED, WHEN DO YOU DECIDE TO GIVE UP?

ONCE YOUR FRIENDS, YOUR FAMILY, AND THE PEOPLE WHO BEAT YOU UP IN HIGH SCHOOL HAVE LABELED YOU AS A SUCCESSFUL PERSON, WOULD YOU STILL RISK FAILING PUBLICLY ON A NEW PROJECT?

HOW DO YOU MAKE SURE THAT SUCCESS GIVES YOU MORE FREEDOM, NOT LESS?

ARE YOU A WORKAHOLIC?

DO YOU EVER SAY NO TO NEW WORK?

WHY DO YOU THINK THAT IS?

DOES WORK ALWAYS MAGICALLY TAKE EXACTLY AS MUCH TIME AS YOU HAVE?

DOES ANYBODY BELIEVE YOU WHEN YOU SAY, "I WISH I HAD MORE FREE TIME"?

WHEN YOU HAVE FREE TIME, DO YOU COME UP WITH BIG NEW PROJECTS FOR YOURSELF?

LIKE, SAY, A BOOK OF QUESTIONS?

WHEN DID YOU FIRST NOTICE IT?

OR DRAWING A MONSTER A DAY?

WHO ARE YOU WORKING TO KEEP OUT?

OR . . . NAME YOUR POISON?

ARE YOU DOING IT CONSCIOUSLY?

OR IS THERE ANOTHER REASON YOU'RE WORKING TO THE EXCLUSION OF MOST OR ALL OTHER THINGS?

ARE YOU BEING HONEST ABOUT IT WITH THE PEOPLE IN YOUR LIFE?

OR IS THE WHOLE POINT OF WORKING AS MUCH AS YOU DO THAT IT KEEPS YOU FROM HAVING TO BE HONEST WITH THE PEOPLE IN YOUR LIFE?

WHAT'S THE HOLE YOU'RE TRYING TO FILL WITH YOUR ACHIEVEMENTS?

OR WITH YOURSELF?

OR IS IT REALLY, TRULY JUST THAT YOU'RE BETTER AT WORK THAN AT ANYTHING ELSE, AND THAT IT MAKES YOU HAPPY TO CREATE THINGS?

102

HOW HAS IT BEEN USEFUL TO YOU?

ARE YOUR SYMPTOMS MANAGEABLE? ➔ FOR YOU? ➔ FOR THE PEOPLE AROUND YOU?

DO YOU **WANT** TO CHANGE? ➔ DO **YOU** WANT TO CHANGE? ➔ ARE YOU HAVING FUN?

IF THERE'S NO PROBLEM, THEN WHAT'S THE PROBLEM?

IF THERE IS A PROBLEM, WHAT CAN YOU DO TO CUT BACK WITHOUT LOSING YOUR EDGE?

IS IT POSSIBLE TO CUT BACK WITHOUT LOSING YOUR EDGE?

ARE YOU WILLING TO COMPROMISE? ➔ WHO WILL YOU RESENT FOR THIS?

OR IS THERE A CHANCE YOU MIGHT BE GRATEFUL?

INCIDENTALLY, SHOULD WE GET TOGETHER SOMETIME AND GROUSE ABOUT PEOPLE WHO GO ON AND ON ABOUT HOW NOBODY EVER LOOKS BACK AT THEIR LIFE WISHING THEY'D SPENT MORE TIME AT THEIR DESK?

NEXT MONTH? NO GOOD? IN THE FALL? POSSIBLY? WHEN DO YOU HAVE SOMETHING OPEN? DO YOU JUST WANNA PLAY IT BY EAR FOR NOW?

WHAT DID WE ASK AUTHOR AND EDUCATION ACTIVIST

DAVE EGGERS

QUESTION MARK

What questions do you wish somebody had asked you when you were a student?

WHAT IF YOU JUST USE A FEW FONTS PER PAGE, AS OPPOSED TO 12?

How about if you make the type readable?

DO YOU THINK THIS PHOTO, WHICH TURNED OUT BLACK IN THE NEWSPAPER, COULD HAVE BEEN PRINTED BETTER?

DO YOU THINK YOU USE YOUR OWN HANDWRITING TOO MUCH IN YOUR WORK?

What questions do you wish somebody had asked you a year ago?

Would you consider using a font other than Garamond 3?

DO YOU THINK YOU'VE EXHAUSTED THE IDEA OF TYPE SET ON A RADIAL DESIGN?

103

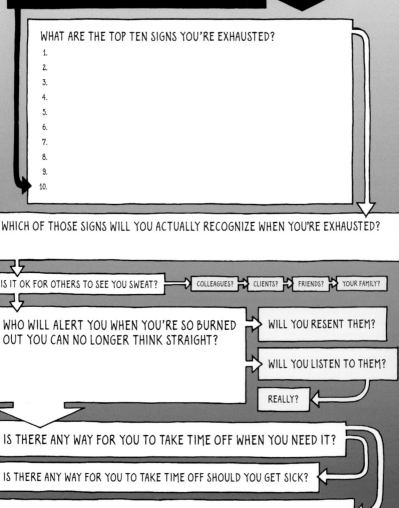

WHAT DO YOU DO WHEN YOU'VE EXHAUSTED YOURSELF?

WHAT ARE THE TOP TEN SIGNS YOU'RE EXHAUSTED?
1.
2.
3.
4.
5.
6.
7.
8.
9.
10.

WHICH OF THOSE SIGNS WILL YOU ACTUALLY RECOGNIZE WHEN YOU'RE EXHAUSTED?

IS IT OK FOR OTHERS TO SEE YOU SWEAT? → COLLEAGUES? → CLIENTS? → FRIENDS? → YOUR FAMILY?

WHO WILL ALERT YOU WHEN YOU'RE SO BURNED OUT YOU CAN NO LONGER THINK STRAIGHT?

WILL YOU RESENT THEM?

WILL YOU LISTEN TO THEM?

REALLY?

IS THERE ANY WAY FOR YOU TO TAKE TIME OFF WHEN YOU NEED IT?

IS THERE ANY WAY FOR YOU TO TAKE TIME OFF SHOULD YOU GET SICK?

WHAT HAPPENS IF YOU HAVE AN ACCIDENT?

IF YOU CUT YOURSELF YOU STOP WHAT YOU'RE DOING, RIGHT?

BECAUSE OF THE PAIN AND THE BLOOD, CORRECT?

BUT EXHAUSTION ISN'T EVER THAT URGENT, IS IT?

IF YOU HAD TO ASSIGN PERCENTAGES, HOW MUCH OF YOUR INCOME IS BASED ON YOUR HANDS AND HOW MUCH ON YOUR HEAD?

0   10   20   30   40   50   60   70   80   90   100

WHAT'S YOUR EMERGENCY PLAN FOR TAKING TIME OFF TO LET YOURSELF GET SOME REST AND RELAXATION?

DO YOU CARE THAT I'M BEING A TOTAL HYPOCRITE RIGHT NOW?

DOES BEING A BAD EXAMPLE GIVE ME ANY CREDIBILITY?

WHAT IF WE MAKE SOME CHANGES TOGETHER?

ON 3?   →   1?   →   2?   →   3?   →   WELL, DID **YOU** DO IT?

STEFAN SAGMEISTER

DO YOU WORK AT HOME OR IN AN OFFICE?

ARE YOU KEEPING REGULAR WORKING HOURS?

HOW MANY HOURS DO YOU WORK A WEEK?

AT NIGHT, DO YOU DREAM OF WORK? IF YES, TELL ME ABOUT THOSE DREAMS.

ANY NIGHTMARES?

HOW MANY OF YOUR FRIENDS ARE IN A COMPLETELY DIFFERENT PROFESSION AS YOU?

DO YOU ANSWER EMAILS ON YOUR HOLIDAYS?

WHAT DO YOU DO WHEN YOU FIRST GET UP IN THE MORNING?

ANSWER EMAIL?

KISS YOUR PARTNER?

OF THE LAST 10 BOOKS YOU LOOKED AT, HOW MANY WERE DESIGN BOOKS?

WHAT IF YOU WERE TO GIVE YOUR SANITY A NAME?

WOULD IT CHANGE ANYTHING IF YOU SAID, "I HAVEN'T REALLY CONSIDERED STEVE IN ANY OF MY PLANS." OR "I DIDN'T REALLY THINK HOW TAKING THIS JOB WOULD AFFECT RUBY"?

DO YOU VALUE YOUR SANITY?

HOW MUCH MONEY WOULD YOU LOSE IF YOU HAD A NERVOUS BREAKDOWN?

HOW MUCH TIME WOULD YOU LOSE?

HOW MUCH DID IT COST YOU LAST TIME?

IS IT TAKING YOU LONGER TO RECOVER THAN IT USED TO?

WHAT ARE THE THINGS THAT KEEP YOU SANE?

HOW CAN YOU ESTABLISH SACROSANCT BOUNDARIES TO DO THOSE THINGS?

DO YOU NEED AN EXCUSE?

BEYOND THE LAST THREE PAGES?

HOW ABOUT "A STITCH IN TIME SAVES NINE?"

HAVE YOU EVER BEEN SERIOUSLY ILL?

IF YOU HAVEN'T, OR HAVEN'T BEEN NEAR SERIOUS ILLNESS, DO YOU THINK THAT MAKES YOU MORE AFRAID OR LESS?

HOW DID THAT CHANGE YOU?

DO YOU VALUE YOUR HEALTH?

IS YOUR BODY A TOY, A TOOL, OR A STORAGE DEVICE?

DO YOU TREAT IT WITH AS MUCH CARE AND RESPECT AS THE REST OF YOUR PERSONAL PROPERTY?

HOW DO YOUR IDEAS CHANGE WHEN YOUR BODY CHANGES?

HOW TIRED DO YOU HAVE TO BE TO HAVE CRAZY IDEAS?

HOW TIRED DO YOU HAVE TO BE FOR CRAZY IDEAS TO BECOME USELESS IDEAS?

IS A GREAT IDEA WORTH GETTING SICK?

IS A GREAT IDEA WORTH GETTING SO SICK THAT YOU MISS OUT ON THE NEXT IDEA AFTER THAT?

HOW MUCH IS A GREAT IDEA WORTH?

HOW QUICKLY WILL YOU GET BETTER?

HOW MUCH WILL BEING SICK COST YOU?

HOW DO YOU KNOW YOU'RE GETTING SICK?

WHAT DO YOU DO, IF ANYTHING, WHEN YOU START FEELING LIKE THAT?

HOW DO YOU KNOW YOU'RE GETTING SICK IF YOU WON'T REALLY FEEL IT
FOR ANOTHER TEN OR TWENTY YEARS?

DO YOU CARE? → DO YOU THINK YOU'LL CARE WHEN IT ACTUALLY HAPPENS?

WHAT'S THE MOST HARMFUL THING YOU'RE DOING TO YOUR BODY RIGHT NOW?

→ DO YOU DO IT BECAUSE IT BRINGS YOU PLEASURE?

→ OR BECAUSE IT LETS YOU DO THE WORK YOU WANT TO DO?

→ OR IS IT JUST FORCE OF HABIT?

WHAT ARE THE FIVE EASIEST WAYS TO STAY HEALTHY WITHOUT TAKING UP TOO MUCH OF YOUR TIME?

1.

2.

3.

4.

5.

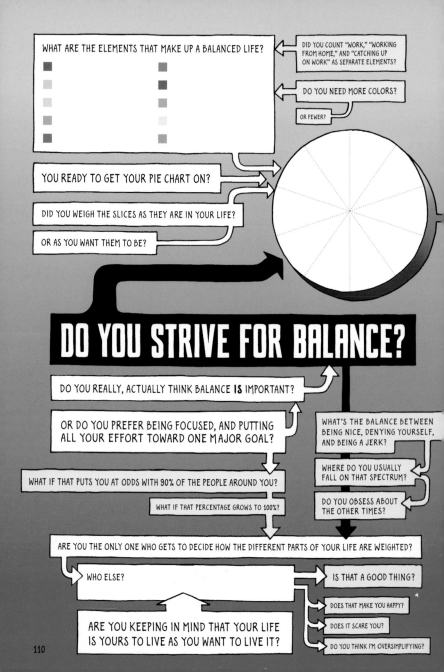

WHAT ARE THE ELEMENTS THAT MAKE UP A BALANCED LIFE?

DID YOU COUNT "WORK," "WORKING FROM HOME," AND "CATCHING UP ON WORK" AS SEPARATE ELEMENTS?

DO YOU NEED MORE COLORS?

OR FEWER?

YOU READY TO GET YOUR PIE CHART ON?

DID YOU WEIGH THE SLICES AS THEY ARE IN YOUR LIFE?

OR AS YOU WANT THEM TO BE?

DO YOU STRIVE FOR BALANCE?

DO YOU REALLY, ACTUALLY THINK BALANCE **IS** IMPORTANT?

OR DO YOU PREFER BEING FOCUSED, AND PUTTING ALL YOUR EFFORT TOWARD ONE MAJOR GOAL?

WHAT'S THE BALANCE BETWEEN BEING NICE, DENYING YOURSELF, AND BEING A JERK?

WHERE DO YOU USUALLY FALL ON THAT SPECTRUM?

WHAT IF THAT PUTS YOU AT ODDS WITH 90% OF THE PEOPLE AROUND YOU?

WHAT IF THAT PERCENTAGE GROWS TO 100%?

DO YOU OBSESS ABOUT THE OTHER TIMES?

ARE YOU THE ONLY ONE WHO GETS TO DECIDE HOW THE DIFFERENT PARTS OF YOUR LIFE ARE WEIGHTED?

WHO ELSE?

IS THAT A GOOD THING?

DOES THAT MAKE YOU HAPPY?

ARE YOU KEEPING IN MIND THAT YOUR LIFE IS YOURS TO LIVE AS YOU WANT TO LIVE IT?

DOES IT SCARE YOU?

DO YOU THINK I'M OVERSIMPLIFYING?

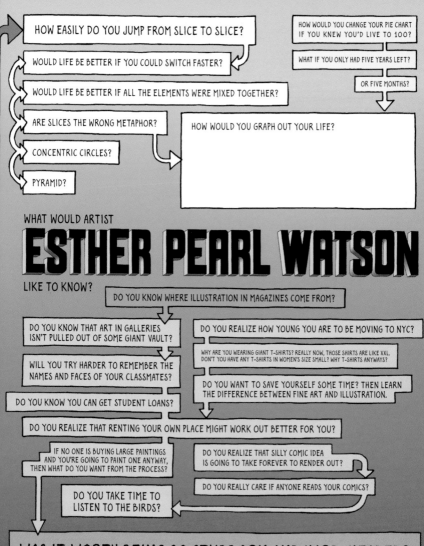

HOW EASILY DO YOU JUMP FROM SLICE TO SLICE?

WOULD LIFE BE BETTER IF YOU COULD SWITCH FASTER?

WOULD LIFE BE BETTER IF ALL THE ELEMENTS WERE MIXED TOGETHER?

ARE SLICES THE WRONG METAPHOR?

CONCENTRIC CIRCLES?

PYRAMID?

HOW WOULD YOU CHANGE YOUR PIE CHART IF YOU KNEW YOU'D LIVE TO 100?

WHAT IF YOU ONLY HAD FIVE YEARS LEFT?

OR FIVE MONTHS?

HOW WOULD YOU GRAPH OUT YOUR LIFE?

WHAT WOULD ARTIST

ESTHER PEARL WATSON

LIKE TO KNOW?

DO YOU KNOW WHERE ILLUSTRATION IN MAGAZINES COME FROM?

DO YOU KNOW THAT ART IN GALLERIES ISN'T PULLED OUT OF SOME GIANT VAULT?

DO YOU REALIZE HOW YOUNG YOU ARE TO BE MOVING TO NYC?

WHY ARE YOU WEARING GIANT T-SHIRTS? REALLY NOW, THOSE SHIRTS ARE LIKE XXL. DON'T YOU HAVE ANY T-SHIRTS IN WOMEN'S SIZE SMALL? WHY T-SHIRTS ANYWAYS?

WILL YOU TRY HARDER TO REMEMBER THE NAMES AND FACES OF YOUR CLASSMATES?

DO YOU WANT TO SAVE YOURSELF SOME TIME? THEN LEARN THE DIFFERENCE BETWEEN FINE ART AND ILLUSTRATION.

DO YOU KNOW YOU CAN GET STUDENT LOANS?

DO YOU REALIZE THAT RENTING YOUR OWN PLACE MIGHT WORK OUT BETTER FOR YOU?

IF NO ONE IS BUYING LARGE PAINTINGS AND YOU'RE GOING TO PAINT ONE ANYWAY, THEN WHAT DO YOU WANT FROM THE PROCESS?

DO YOU REALIZE THAT SILLY COMIC IDEA IS GOING TO TAKE FOREVER TO RENDER OUT?

DO YOU TAKE TIME TO LISTEN TO THE BIRDS?

DO YOU REALLY CARE IF ANYONE READS YOUR COMICS?

WAS IT WORTH BEING SO STUBBORN AND HARD-HEADED?

EVEN THOUGH YOU'RE BUSY AND TIRED, WILL YOU TRY TO SPEND MORE TIME WITH FRIENDS?

HAVE YOU SEEN ANY GOOD "BAD" PAINTINGS LATELY?

DID YOU TAKE TIME OUT TO PLAY WITH YOUR DAUGHTER?

WHAT ARE YOU PAINTING NOW?

WHEN SOMEBODY ASKS YOU WHAT YOU'RE MOST PROUD OF, WHAT'S YOUR FIRST THOUGHT?

AND WHAT'S THE ANSWER YOU GIVE THEM?

IF THE ANSWER YOU GIVE IS DIFFERENT FROM THE ANSWER IN YOUR HEAD, WHY DO YOU THINK THAT IS?

WHAT ARE YOUR PRIORITIES?

DO YOU PLACE MORE VALUE ON YOUR WORK OR ON THE REST OF YOUR LIFE?

IF YOU HAD TO CHOOSE YOUR WORK OR YOUR FRIENDS, WHAT WOULD YOU CHOOSE?

IF YOU HAD TO CHOOSE YOUR WORK OR YOUR PARTNER, WHAT WOULD YOU CHOOSE?

IF YOU HAD TO CHOOSE YOUR WORK OR YOUR FAMILY, WHAT WOULD YOU CHOOSE?

IF YOU HAD TO CHOOSE YOUR WORK OR YOUR HEALTH, WHAT WOULD YOU CHOOSE?

DO YOU THINK YOU CAN HAVE ALL OF THOSE THINGS WITHOUT COMPROMISING YOUR WORK?

DO YOU THINK YOU CAN HAVE ALL OF THOSE THINGS WITHOUT SHORT-CHANGING THE PEOPLE IN YOUR LIFE?

DO YOU THINK YOU DESERVE ALL OF THOSE THINGS?

WHY NOT?

LYNDA WEINMAN

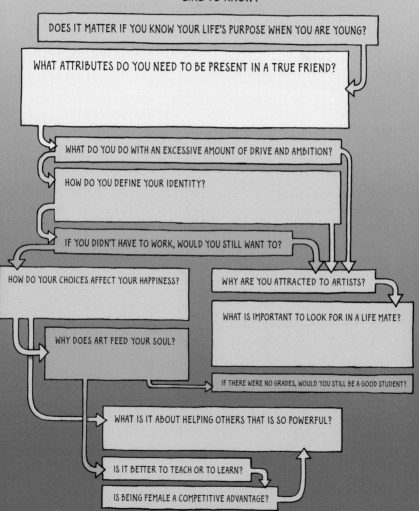

DOES IT MATTER IF YOU KNOW YOUR LIFE'S PURPOSE WHEN YOU ARE YOUNG?

WHAT ATTRIBUTES DO YOU NEED TO BE PRESENT IN A TRUE FRIEND?

WHAT DO YOU DO WITH AN EXCESSIVE AMOUNT OF DRIVE AND AMBITION?

HOW DO YOU DEFINE YOUR IDENTITY?

IF YOU DIDN'T HAVE TO WORK, WOULD YOU STILL WANT TO?

HOW DO YOUR CHOICES AFFECT YOUR HAPPINESS?

WHY ARE YOU ATTRACTED TO ARTISTS?

WHAT IS IMPORTANT TO LOOK FOR IN A LIFE MATE?

WHY DOES ART FEED YOUR SOUL?

IF THERE WERE NO GRADES, WOULD YOU STILL BE A GOOD STUDENT?

WHAT IS IT ABOUT HELPING OTHERS THAT IS SO POWERFUL?

IS IT BETTER TO TEACH OR TO LEARN?

IS BEING FEMALE A COMPETITIVE ADVANTAGE?

HAVE YOU OPENED YOUR HEART TO QUESTIONS FROM

BOB DUCCA

DIVORCED MAN, PROUD EX-STEP FATHER, SUFFERER OF AILMENTS, VICTIM OF ALLERGIES, AND HOBBYIST?

DO YOU DO THINGS SLOWLY?

ARE YOU HAVING DIFFICULTY MAKING DECISIONS?

HAVE YOU LOST INTEREST IN ASPECTS OF YOUR LIFE THAT USED TO BE OF INTEREST TO YOU?

WAIT, I'M SORRY. I THOUGHT THIS WAS A QUESTIONNAIRE.

IF YOU COULD HUG YOURSELF HOW MANY RIBS WOULD YOU BREAK?

WHO WOULD WIN IN A FIGHT, YOUR EGO OR YOUR FEAR?

WHEN IS THE LAST TIME YOU LOOKED INTO A MIRROR AND SAID **I LOVE YOU?**

DO YOU EVER FEAR THAT WHILE LOOKING INTO A MIRROR A GOLLUM OR OTHER TYPE OF MONSTER WILL BE BEHIND YOU?

DO YOU EVER CRY SO HARD IN THE SELF-HELP SECTION OF BARNES & NOBLE THAT YOU KNOCK OVER YOUR EXTRA LARGE COFFEE THAT YOU BOUGHT BECAUSE YOU PLANNED TO STAY THERE ALL DAY UNTIL YOUR LIFE WAS FIXED?

MAY I PLEASE HAVE A RIDE TO BARNES & NOBLE?

WHAT'S THE LONELIEST YOU'VE EVER BEEN?

WANNA BET I CAN TOP IT?

DO YOU HAVE ANY HOBBIES?

DO YOU HAVE ANY HOBBIES THAT REQUIRE A PARTNER?

ARE YOU AWARE THAT WE ONLY USE 10% OF OUR BRAIN?

MAY I BE YOUR HOBBY PARTNER?

DO YOU FIND THAT FACT, AS I DO, TO BE A COMFORTING EXCUSE FOR WHERE YOUR LIFE HAS ENDED UP?

IF YOU WERE ONE OF PIONEERING SELF-HELP AUTHOR SHAKTI GAWAIN'S **DAILY AFFIRMATIONS,** WHICH ONE WOULD YOU BE?

WHEN IS THE LAST TIME YOU DANCED AS IF NO ONE WAS LOOKING?

ARE YOU EVER CONCERNED THAT SOMEONE MAY HAVE SECRETLY PLACED A NANNY-CAM IN YOUR APARTMENT?

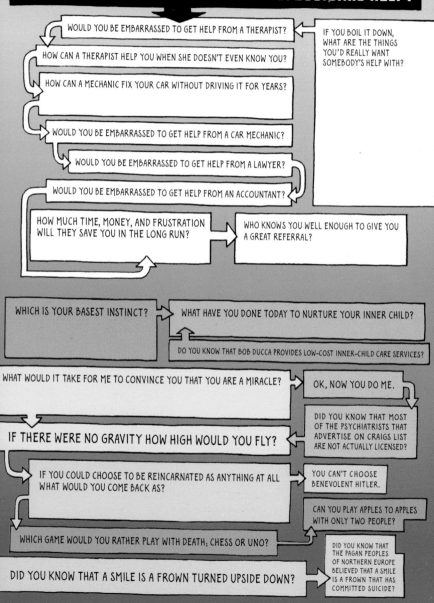

IS IT OK IF THE HEAD WRITER OF
THE DAILY SHOW WITH JON STEWART

TIM CARVELL

MIXES IN SOME INSTRUCTIONS WITH HIS QUESTIONS?

WHY, EXACTLY, DO YOU FIND THAT FUNNY?

WHAT IS THE FUNNIEST THING YOU CAN IMAGINE?

WHAT WOULD MAKE THAT FUNNIER?

WOULD IT BE FUNNIER IF IT INVOLVED THE WORD "BADGER"?

WRITE DOWN A LIST OF WORDS THAT ARE INHERENTLY FUNNY.
HERE, I'VE ALREADY STARTED IT FOR YOU:

1. **BANJO**
2.
3.
4.
5.

WHAT IF EVERYONE INVOLVED WERE WEARING HELMETS?

IN A NON-HELMET-REQUIRING-TYPE SITUATION?

WHAT IF IT INVOLVED BADGERS IN HELMETS?

WHAT DO YOU CONSIDER "GOING TOO FAR," COMEDY-WISE?

WRITE DOWN A FAVORITE JOKE OF YOURS:

IN TERMS OF "GOING TOO FAR," DOES IT MAKE A DIFFERENCE WHO'S TELLING THE JOKE?

WHY?

OK, NOW: IMAGINE THAT JOKE ACTUALLY HAPPENING TO YOU, IN REAL LIFE. WOULD IT STILL BE FUNNY?

OR WOULD IT BE HORRIFYING?

THE LINE BETWEEN COMEDY AND TRAGEDY, IT'S OFTEN BEEN SAID, IS VERY FINE. PICK ONE OF THE FOLLOWING TRAGEDIES AND FIGURE OUT WHAT IT'D TAKE TO TURN IT INTO A COMEDY.

OEDIPUS REX → MEDEA → HAMLET

ROMEO AND JULIET → DEATH OF A SALESMAN

NOTE: TRY TURNING THE MAIN CHARACTER INTO A BADGER WEARING A HELMET!

116

WHAT'S FUNNY TO YOU?

DO YOU THINK LIFE IS FUNNY?

WHEN YOU REALLY LOOK AT IT?

CAN YOU STOP TAKING THINGS SERIOUSLY, BUT STILL ACT RESPONSIBLY?

KEEPING IN MIND THAT THE METER IS RUNNING FOR ALL OF US?

WHAT IF YOU DIDN'T HAVE TO WORRY ABOUT THE AFTERLIFE?

WHAT ARE THE THINGS THAT WEIGH HEAVIEST ON YOUR MIND RIGHT NOW?

DO YOU THINK ANY OF THAT WILL MAKE FOR A FUNNY STORY IN A FEW YEARS?

CAN YOU ACCELERATE THAT PROCESS?

DO YOU WORRY ABOUT EMBARRASSING YOURSELF?

NEXT TIME YOU DO, CAN YOU WEAVE IT INTO A GOOD STORY BEFORE ANYBODY ELSE?

WHAT IF SOMEBODY BEATS YOU TO IT?

WHAT PISSES YOU OFF EVERY DAMN DAY?

WHY?

REALLY?

DON'T YOU THINK THAT'S KINDA FUNNY?

DO YOU EQUATE GROWING UP WITH GETTING SERIOUS?

WHAT IF IT'S THE EXACT OPPOSITE?

WRITE YOUR OWN KNOCK-KNOCK JOKE HERE:

KNOCK-KNOCK.
WHO'S THERE?

_____

_____ WHO?

_____

_____

HA HA! I'VE NEVER HEARD THAT ONE BEFORE!

WOULD YOUR WORK BE BETTER IF IT WERE FUNNIER?

WOULD YOU HAVE MORE FUN DOING YOUR WORK?

WOULD THAT MAKE YOU A BETTER PERSON?

KINDER TO PEOPLE AND PUPPIES ALIKE?

117

HOW LONG HAS THIS BEEN GOING ON?

IS IT THAT YOU DON'T HAVE ANY IDEAS?

OR IS IT THAT YOU DON'T HAVE ANY IDEAS THAT YOU THINK ARE ANY GOOD?

ARE YOU OPEN TO THE POSSIBILITY THAT YOU MIGHT BE WRONG ABOUT THAT?

OR THAT A LAME START IS STILL A START AND CAN LEAD TO GREAT RESULTS?

HOW DO YOU BREAK THROUGH CREATIVE BLOCK?

IS IT REALLY A CREATIVE BLOCK, OR IS IT THAT YOU CAN'T BRING YOURSELF TO SIT AT YOUR DESK AND START WORKING?

CAN YOU PROCRASTINATE ON ONE JOB WITH ANOTHER ONE?

HOW LONG DOES IT USUALLY TAKE UNTIL THE SHAME OF NOT WORKING OUTWEIGHS THE ANXIETY OF COMING UP WITH IDEAS?

ARE THERE GRUNT WORK PARTS OF THE JOB YOU CAN DO FIRST?

WHAT IS IT THAT REALLY SCARES YOU ABOUT THE WORK AT HAND?

SET UP THE FILE?

ORGANIZE AND FORMAT IMAGES?

TAKE SOME SCRAP PHOTOS?

IS IT THAT THIS IS THE JOB THAT WILL FINALLY EXPOSE YOU AS THE FRAUD YOU KNOW YOU ARE?

OR IS IT REALLY JUST YOU vs. THE WHITE PAGE?

IS IT THAT YOU'RE PHYSICALLY EXHAUSTED?

ARE HARD DRUGS REALLY A VIABLE OPTION?

IS YOUR MIND ELSEWHERE?

OR A CAREER IN BEE-KEEPING?

CAN YOU USE SOME NEW TOOLS?

WHAT CAN YOU DO TO PUT DOWN SOMETHING, ANYTHING, TO UN-PERFECT THAT WHITE PAGE?

CAN YOU USE SOME OLD TOOLS?

CAN YOU HAVE SOMEBODY ELSE MAKE THAT FIRST MARK, OR WRITE THAT FIRST SENTENCE?

IF ALL ELSE FAILS, CAN YOU CALL A FRIEND FOR HELP?

CAN YOU PRETEND TO BE THAT OTHER PERSON?

CHRISTOPH NIEMANN

IS THERE TIME FOR ANOTHER COFFEE?

WHAT IS THE CREATIVE PROBLEM YOU ARE TRYING TO SOLVE?

IS YOUR IDEA OF THE CREATIVE PROBLEM THE SAME AS YOUR CLIENT'S IDEA OF THE PROBLEM?

CAN YOU REPHRASE IT IN THREE SENTENCES?

WHAT ELEMENTS SHOULD YOUR SOLUTION **NOT** CONTAIN?

WHAT WOULD A STUPID, SIMPLE, UNCREATIVE BUT WORKABLE SOLUTION LOOK LIKE?

WHO IS THE PROTOTYPICAL READER/USER WHO SHOULD BE IMPRESSED BY YOUR WORK?
(FRIEND? COLLEAGUE? MOM? HERO?)

WHAT REACTION SHOULD READERS/USERS HAVE WHEN THEY SEE YOUR WORK
(DESIRE TO LAUGH, THINK, ACT, PURCHASE)?

WILL BROWSING THE WWW REALLY INSPIRE YOU OR KEEP YOU FROM ACTUALLY TACKLING YOUR CREATIVE PROBLEM?

IS THERE TIME FOR YET ANOTHER COFFEE?

ARE YOU A VIRTUOSO?

WOULD YOU LIKE TO BE A VIRTUOSO?

OR A JACK OF ALL TRADES?

WHAT DO YOU THINK IT TAKES TO BE ONE?

WHAT DO YOU THINK IT TAKES TO BE ONE?

WHAT WOULD BE FUN ABOUT IT FOR YOU?

WHAT WOULD BE FUN ABOUT IT FOR YOU?

WHAT WOULD YOU HAVE TO GIVE UP IN EXCHANGE?

WHAT WOULD YOU HAVE TO GIVE UP IN EXCHANGE?

HOW CAN YOU WALK DOWN TWO STREETS AT ONCE?

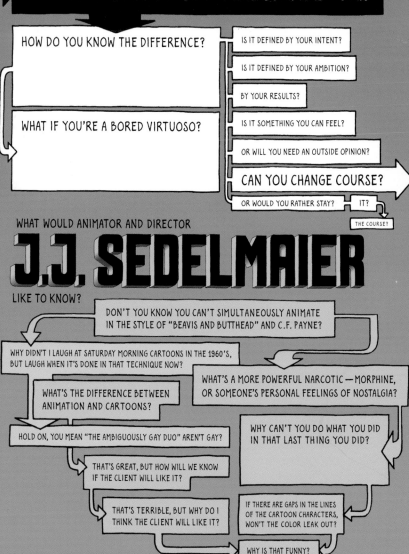

OR DO YOU JUST DO THE SAME THING OVER AND OVER?

HOW DO YOU KNOW THE DIFFERENCE?

IS IT DEFINED BY YOUR INTENT?

IS IT DEFINED BY YOUR AMBITION?

BY YOUR RESULTS?

WHAT IF YOU'RE A BORED VIRTUOSO?

IS IT SOMETHING YOU CAN FEEL?

OR WILL YOU NEED AN OUTSIDE OPINION?

CAN YOU CHANGE COURSE?

OR WOULD YOU RATHER STAY? IT?

THE COURSE?

WHAT WOULD ANIMATOR AND DIRECTOR

J.J. SEDELMAIER

LIKE TO KNOW?

DON'T YOU KNOW YOU CAN'T SIMULTANEOUSLY ANIMATE IN THE STYLE OF "BEAVIS AND BUTTHEAD" AND C.F. PAYNE?

WHY DIDN'T I LAUGH AT SATURDAY MORNING CARTOONS IN THE 1960'S, BUT LAUGH WHEN IT'S DONE IN THAT TECHNIQUE NOW?

WHAT'S A MORE POWERFUL NARCOTIC — MORPHINE, OR SOMEONE'S PERSONAL FEELINGS OF NOSTALGIA?

WHAT'S THE DIFFERENCE BETWEEN ANIMATION AND CARTOONS?

HOLD ON, YOU MEAN "THE AMBIGUOUSLY GAY DUO" AREN'T GAY?

WHY CAN'T YOU DO WHAT YOU DID IN THAT LAST THING YOU DID?

THAT'S GREAT, BUT HOW WILL WE KNOW IF THE CLIENT WILL LIKE IT?

THAT'S TERRIBLE, BUT WHY DO I THINK THE CLIENT WILL LIKE IT?

IF THERE ARE GAPS IN THE LINES OF THE CARTOON CHARACTERS, WON'T THE COLOR LEAK OUT?

WHY IS THAT FUNNY?

121

DID YOU MAKE A CONSCIOUS DECISION TO STOP LEARNING?

IF YOUR FAVORITE BAND STOPS RECORDING NEW MUSIC, BUT KEEPS TOURING, HOW OFTEN WILL YOU GO TO THEIR SHOWS BEFORE IT'S JUST TOO SAD?

WHAT'S YOUR VERSION OF RECORDING A DOUBLE ALBUM OF MOTOWN COVERS WITH A BIG BAND?

HOW DO YOU KEEP

WHERE CAN YOU LEARN SOMETHING **IMPORTANT** TODAY?

WHO'LL TEACH YOU SOMETHING ON THE DAYS WHEN YOU DON'T WANT TO LEARN ANYTHING?

WHERE CAN YOU LEARN SOMETHING **USEFUL** TODAY?

WHAT WOULD COMEDIAN, AUTHOR, AND ACTOR

PATTON OSWALT

LIKE TO KNOW?

ARE YOU LEARNING TO EXPLAIN WHAT YOU LIKE AS CLEARLY AS YOU CAN EXPLAIN WHAT YOU DON'T?

CAN YOU IMAGINE WHAT YOUR TEACHERS MIGHT HAVE BEEN LIKE AT YOUR AGE?

What questions do you wish somebody had asked you when you were a student?

CAN YOU IMAGINE WHAT YOU MIGHT BE LIKE AT THEIR AGE?

ARE THERE THINGS YOU'RE STARTING TO SUSPECT YOU'RE NEVER GOING TO WANT TO DO?

WHAT DO YOU THINK IS MORE VALUABLE—FREEDOM OR PEACE?

122

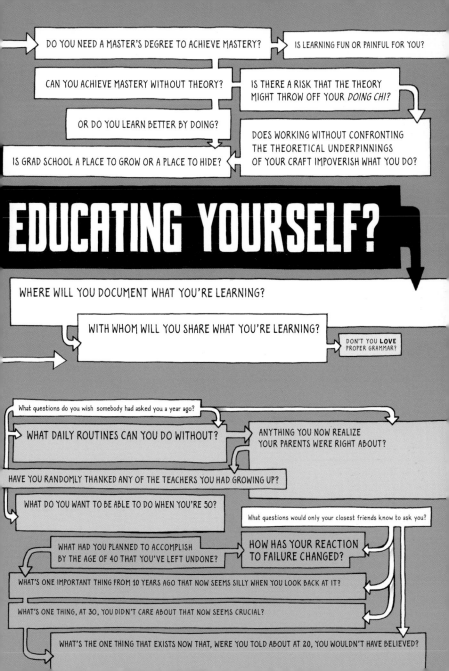

DO YOU NEED A MASTER'S DEGREE TO ACHIEVE MASTERY?

IS LEARNING FUN OR PAINFUL FOR YOU?

CAN YOU ACHIEVE MASTERY WITHOUT THEORY?

IS THERE A RISK THAT THE THEORY MIGHT THROW OFF YOUR *DOING CHI*?

OR DO YOU LEARN BETTER BY DOING?

DOES WORKING WITHOUT CONFRONTING THE THEORETICAL UNDERPINNINGS OF YOUR CRAFT IMPOVERISH WHAT YOU DO?

IS GRAD SCHOOL A PLACE TO GROW OR A PLACE TO HIDE?

EDUCATING YOURSELF?

WHERE WILL YOU DOCUMENT WHAT YOU'RE LEARNING?

WITH WHOM WILL YOU SHARE WHAT YOU'RE LEARNING?

DON'T YOU **LOVE** PROPER GRAMMAR?

What questions do you wish somebody had asked you a year ago?

WHAT DAILY ROUTINES CAN YOU DO WITHOUT?

ANYTHING YOU NOW REALIZE YOUR PARENTS WERE RIGHT ABOUT?

HAVE YOU RANDOMLY THANKED ANY OF THE TEACHERS YOU HAD GROWING UP?

WHAT DO YOU WANT TO BE ABLE TO DO WHEN YOU'RE 50?

What questions would only your closest friends know to ask you?

WHAT HAD YOU PLANNED TO ACCOMPLISH BY THE AGE OF 40 THAT YOU'VE LEFT UNDONE?

HOW HAS YOUR REACTION TO FAILURE CHANGED?

WHAT'S ONE IMPORTANT THING FROM 10 YEARS AGO THAT NOW SEEMS SILLY WHEN YOU LOOK BACK AT IT?

WHAT'S ONE THING, AT 30, YOU DIDN'T CARE ABOUT THAT NOW SEEMS CRUCIAL?

WHAT'S THE ONE THING THAT EXISTS NOW THAT, WERE YOU TOLD ABOUT AT 20, YOU WOULDN'T HAVE BELIEVED?

WHAT WOULD AUTHOR, ARTIST, PRODUCER, AND **CATDOG** CREATOR

PETER HANNAN

LIKE TO KNOW?

WHY ARE YOU A STUDENT?

WHY THIS SCHOOL?

WHAT ARE THE BEST THINGS TO LEARN IN SCHOOL AND THE BEST THINGS TO LEARN OUT OF SCHOOL?

WHAT ARE YOUR 100 FAVORITE THINGS IN THE WORLD?

1.
2.
3.
4.
5.
6.
7.
8.
9.
10.
11.
12.
13.
14.
15.
16.
17.
18.
19.
20.
21.
22.
23.
24.
25.
26.
27.
28.
29.
30.
31.
32.
33.
34.
35.
36.
37.
38.
39.
40.
41.
42.
43.
44.
45.
46.
47.
48.
49.
50.
51.
52.
53.
54.
55.
56.
57.
58.
59.
60.
61.
62.
63.
64.
65.
66.
67.
68.
69.
70.
71.
72.
73.
74.
75.
76.
77.
78.
79.
80.
81.
82.
83.
84.
85.
86.
87.
88.
89.
90.
91.
92.
93.
94.
95.
96.
97.
98.
99.
100.

WHERE WOULD YOU RATHER BE RIGHT NOW?

WHAT PASTIME FEELS LIKE COMING HOME TO YOU?

WHAT ARE YOU DOING TO REALIZE IT?

WHAT'S YOUR GREATEST FEAR?

WHAT ARE YOU DOING TO DESTROY IT?

WHAT SKILL OR TALENT ARE YOU INTRIGUED BY BUT FOR SOME STRANGE REASON FEEL YOU ARE INCAPABLE OF LEARNING OR DOING, BECAUSE YOU FEEL LIKE YOU ARE SOMEHOW UNWORTHY?

WHAT WOULDN'T YOU MIND DOING ALL NIGHT LONG? BESIDES THAT.

WHAT DO YOU LIKE TO DO ON YOUR OWN AND WHAT DO YOU LIKE TO COLLABORATE ON?

WHAT PEOPLE YOU KNOW (OR DON'T KNOW) ARE DOING COOL THINGS WITH THEIR LIVES THAT SEEM LIKE THINGS YOU'D LIKE TO DO, AND WHY HAVEN'T YOU CALLED THOSE PEOPLE YET?

WHY AREN'T YOU A STUDENT?

WHAT ELSE DO YOU WANT TO LEARN?

WHAT PROJECT MIGHT YOU CREATE THAT WILL PAY YOU GOBS OF MONEY TO TRAVEL THE WORLD FOR A FEW YEARS?

DON'T YOU THINK YOU SHOULD GET THAT TOOTH CHECKED OUT?

HOW CAN YOU WORK THINGS OUT SO THAT YOU CAN JUST PLAY MUSIC FOR A YEAR?

HOW CAN YOU WORK THINGS OUT SO THAT YOU CAN JUST WRITE FOR A YEAR?

HOW CAN YOU WORK THINGS OUT SO THAT YOU CAN JUST PAINT FOR A YEAR?

HOW CAN YOU WORK THINGS OUT SO THAT YOU CAN JUST READ FOR A YEAR?

SO WHEN ARE YOU GOING TO START A FREAKING BAND?

SO WHEN ARE YOU GOING TO START A FREAKING SCHOOL?

WHAT'S YOUR LONG-RANGE PLAN?

WHERE ARE YOU GOING WITH ALL THIS?

WHERE DO YOU WANT TO END UP?

ARE YOU SEEING THE FOREST FOR THE TREES?

DO YOU NEED TO BE OUTSIDE THE FOREST TO GRASP ITS MEANING?

DO YOU NEED TO CLIMB ONE OF THE TALLER TREES AND LOOK AROUND?

DO YOU NEED TO STAND IN A CLEARING?

ARE YOU A BOXER?

DO YOU NEED YOUR STORY TOLD MORE OFTEN?

DO YOU NEED A BETTER METAPHOR AND FEWER SIMON & GARFUNKEL PUNS?

WHAT IS THE ONE THING THAT MATTERS TO YOU MORE THAN ANYTHING?

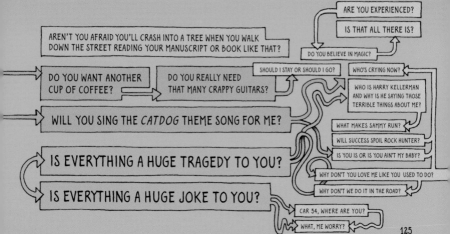

ARE YOU EXPERIENCED?

IS THAT ALL THERE IS?

AREN'T YOU AFRAID YOU'LL CRASH INTO A TREE WHEN YOU WALK
DOWN THE STREET READING YOUR MANUSCRIPT OR BOOK LIKE THAT?

DO YOU BELIEVE IN MAGIC?

DO YOU WANT ANOTHER
CUP OF COFFEE?

DO YOU REALLY NEED
THAT MANY CRAPPY GUITARS?

SHOULD I STAY OR SHOULD I GO?

WHO'S CRYING NOW?

WHO IS HARRY KELLERMAN
AND WHY IS HE SAYING THOSE
TERRIBLE THINGS ABOUT ME?

WILL YOU SING THE *CATDOG* THEME SONG FOR ME?

WHAT MAKES SAMMY RUN?

WILL SUCCESS SPOIL ROCK HUNTER?

IS YOU IS OR IS YOU AIN'T MY BABY?

IS EVERYTHING A HUGE TRAGEDY TO YOU?

WHY DON'T YOU LOVE ME LIKE YOU USED TO DO?

WHY DON'T WE DO IT IN THE ROAD?

IS EVERYTHING A HUGE JOKE TO YOU?

CAR 54, WHERE ARE YOU?

WHAT, ME WORRY?

125

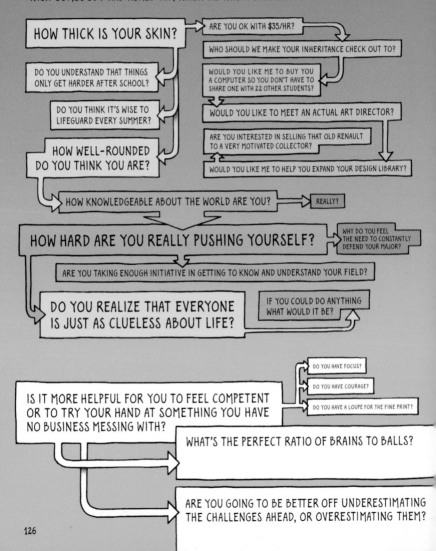

WHAT QUESTIONS DOES DESIGN DIRECTOR OF **THE NEW YORK TIMES MAGAZINE**

AREM DUPLESSIS

WISH SOMEBODY HAD ASKED HIM WHEN HE WAS A STUDENT?

HOW THICK IS YOUR SKIN?

ARE YOU OK WITH $35/HR?

WHO SHOULD WE MAKE YOUR INHERITANCE CHECK OUT TO?

DO YOU UNDERSTAND THAT THINGS ONLY GET HARDER AFTER SCHOOL?

WOULD YOU LIKE ME TO BUY YOU A COMPUTER SO YOU DON'T HAVE TO SHARE ONE WITH 22 OTHER STUDENTS?

DO YOU THINK IT'S WISE TO LIFEGUARD EVERY SUMMER?

WOULD YOU LIKE TO MEET AN ACTUAL ART DIRECTOR?

HOW WELL-ROUNDED DO YOU THINK YOU ARE?

ARE YOU INTERESTED IN SELLING THAT OLD RENAULT TO A VERY MOTIVATED COLLECTOR?

WOULD YOU LIKE ME TO HELP YOU EXPAND YOUR DESIGN LIBRARY?

HOW KNOWLEDGEABLE ABOUT THE WORLD ARE YOU?

REALLY?

HOW HARD ARE YOU REALLY PUSHING YOURSELF?

WHY DO YOU FEEL THE NEED TO CONSTANTLY DEFEND YOUR MAJOR?

ARE YOU TAKING ENOUGH INITIATIVE IN GETTING TO KNOW AND UNDERSTAND YOUR FIELD?

DO YOU REALIZE THAT EVERYONE IS JUST AS CLUELESS ABOUT LIFE?

IF YOU COULD DO ANYTHING WHAT WOULD IT BE?

DO YOU HAVE FOCUS?

DO YOU HAVE COURAGE?

DO YOU HAVE A LOUPE FOR THE FINE PRINT?

IS IT MORE HELPFUL FOR YOU TO FEEL COMPETENT OR TO TRY YOUR HAND AT SOMETHING YOU HAVE NO BUSINESS MESSING WITH?

WHAT'S THE PERFECT RATIO OF BRAINS TO BALLS?

ARE YOU GOING TO BE BETTER OFF UNDERESTIMATING THE CHALLENGES AHEAD, OR OVERESTIMATING THEM?

WHEN DOES IT HELP YOU TO TELL PEOPLE ABOUT YOUR PLANS?

DOES THE SUPPORT OF FRIENDS AND COLLEAGUES KEEP YOU HONEST, SO YOU DON'T ABANDON YOUR IDEA WHEN THINGS GET TRICKY?

WHEN IS IT BETTER TO KEEP THEM TO YOURSELF UNTIL YOU'RE WELL UNDERWAY?

DO YOU GET SO MUCH SATISFACTION FROM TELLING PEOPLE ABOUT AN IDEA THAT THE EXECUTION BECOMES NOTHING MORE THAN A TECHNICALITY?

HOW DO YOU ATTACK THE WORK AHEAD?

CAN YOU BREAK YOUR LONG-RANGE PLAN INTO A LIST OF THINGS YOU CAN START TACKLING TODAY?

WHEN IS THE BEST POINT FOR YOU TO MOVE FROM DREAMING BIG TO GETTING INTO THE DETAILS?

OR DOES THAT MAKE IT FEEL TOO REAL?

WHAT, ARE YOU **CHICKEN?**

WHAT'S THE TO-DO LIST?

HOW DO YOU RECOGNIZE THAT YOU'VE REACHED YOUR GOALS?

WHAT HAPPENS WHEN YOU DO?

WILL YOU TAKE A MOMENT TO ENJOY IT?

WHAT WOULD **FAST COMPANY** COLUMNIST AND GRAPHIC DESIGNER

KEN CARBONE

LIKE TO KNOW?

IS DESIGN ART?

CAN YOU GET RICH AS A GRAPHIC DESIGNER?

DO DESIGNERS HAVE MORE FUN?

WHAT'S MORE IMPORTANT, WORDS OR TYPOGRAPHY?

DO YOU HAVE TO KNOW HOW TO DRAW TO BE A DESIGNER?

DO YOU THINK THERE ARE ANY BAD COLORS?

WHAT'S YOUR DEFINITION OF GOOD DESIGN?

IS IT BETTER TO BE GOOD OR ORIGINAL?

DO YOUR PARENTS KNOW WHAT DESIGNERS DO?

CAN DESIGN CHANGE THE WORLD?

WHAT IS THE BEST BUSINESS MODEL FOR A GRAPHIC DESIGN FIRM?

ARE THERE TOO MANY DESIGNERS?

WHAT ASPECTS OF DESIGN AFFORD THE GREATEST CREATIVE OPPORTUNITY?

WHAT ASPECTS OF DESIGN OFFER THE GREATEST POTENTIAL TO INFLUENCE SOCIETAL CHANGE?

WHAT ASPECTS OF DESIGN OFFER THE GREATEST POTENTIAL TO MAKE MONEY?

IS WINNING DESIGN AWARDS AND PEER RECOGNITION IMPORTANT?

WHAT MAKES A GREAT CLIENT?

WHAT HAPPENS WHEN BAD THINGS HAPPEN TO GOOD DESIGN, i.e. BP?

SHOULD YOU GIVE CLIENTS WHAT THEY WANT, WHAT THEY NEED, OR WHAT THEY DESERVE?

WHAT MAKES A GREAT DESIGN PARTNERSHIP?

WHAT'S THE BEST THING ABOUT A CAREER IN DESIGN?

HOW DO YOU STRIKE THE BALANCE BETWEEN PERSONAL AND PROFESSIONAL LIFE?

WHAT'S THE BEST BALANCE BETWEEN PERSONAL STYLE AND CLIENT NEED?

WHAT'S THE BEST THING ABOUT HAVING YOUR OWN BUSINESS?

WHAT IS THE MOST REWARDING PROJECT YOU HAVE DONE?

WHAT IS YOUR DREAM DESIGN PROJECT?

IF YOU WEREN'T A DESIGNER WHAT WOULD YOU BE?

WHO ARE YOUR DESIGN HEROES?

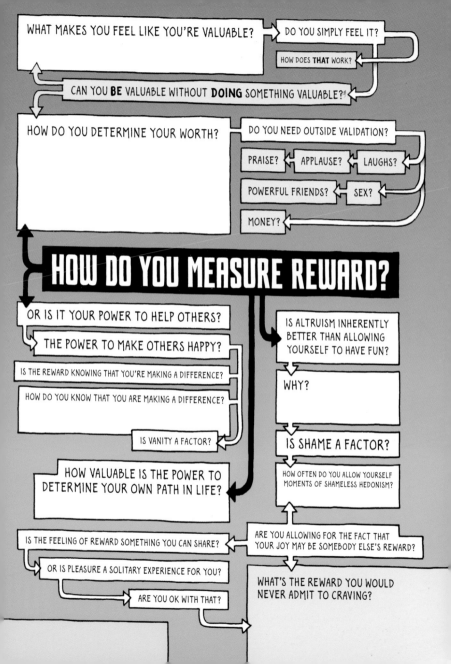

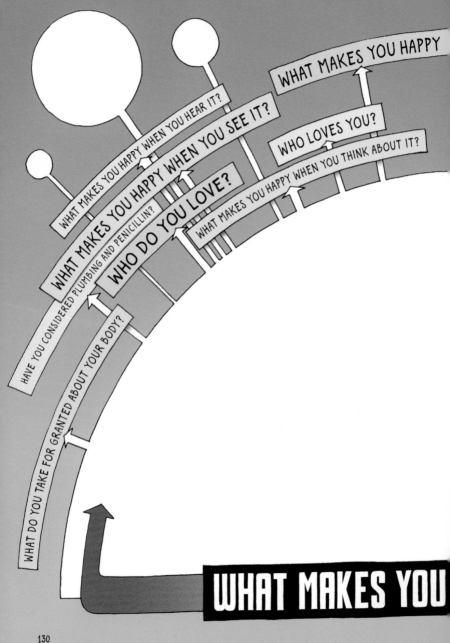

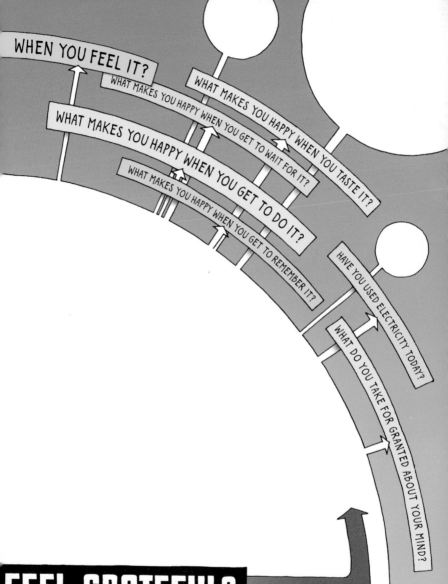

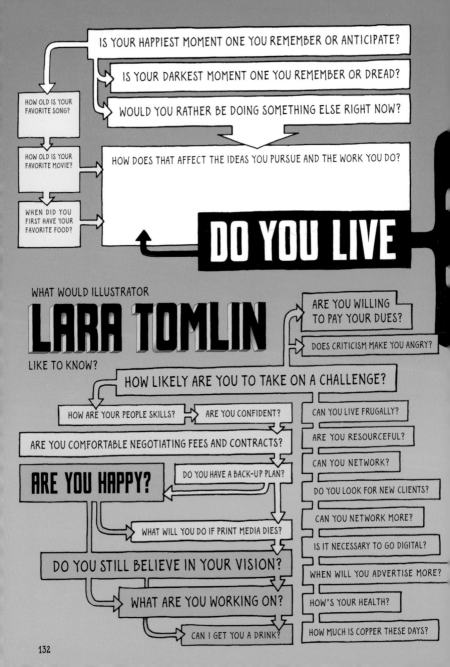

IS YOUR HAPPIEST MOMENT ONE YOU REMEMBER OR ANTICIPATE?

IS YOUR DARKEST MOMENT ONE YOU REMEMBER OR DREAD?

WOULD YOU RATHER BE DOING SOMETHING ELSE RIGHT NOW?

HOW OLD IS YOUR FAVORITE SONG?

HOW OLD IS YOUR FAVORITE MOVIE?

WHEN DID YOU FIRST HAVE YOUR FAVORITE FOOD?

HOW DOES THAT AFFECT THE IDEAS YOU PURSUE AND THE WORK YOU DO?

DO YOU LIVE

WHAT WOULD ILLUSTRATOR

LARA TOMLIN

LIKE TO KNOW?

ARE YOU WILLING TO PAY YOUR DUES?

DOES CRITICISM MAKE YOU ANGRY?

HOW LIKELY ARE YOU TO TAKE ON A CHALLENGE?

HOW ARE YOUR PEOPLE SKILLS?

ARE YOU CONFIDENT?

CAN YOU LIVE FRUGALLY?

ARE YOU RESOURCEFUL?

ARE YOU COMFORTABLE NEGOTIATING FEES AND CONTRACTS?

CAN YOU NETWORK?

ARE YOU HAPPY?

DO YOU HAVE A BACK-UP PLAN?

DO YOU LOOK FOR NEW CLIENTS?

CAN YOU NETWORK MORE?

WHAT WILL YOU DO IF PRINT MEDIA DIES?

IS IT NECESSARY TO GO DIGITAL?

DO YOU STILL BELIEVE IN YOUR VISION?

WHEN WILL YOU ADVERTISE MORE?

WHAT ARE YOU WORKING ON?

HOW'S YOUR HEALTH?

CAN I GET YOU A DRINK?

HOW MUCH IS COPPER THESE DAYS?

132

WHAT WOULD DESIGNER

MARIAN BANTJES

LIKE TO KNOW?

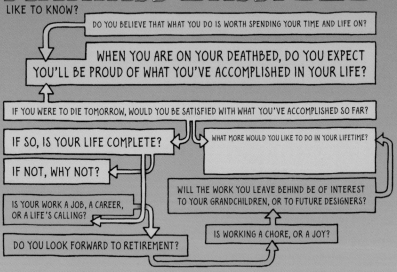

DO YOU BELIEVE THAT WHAT YOU DO IS WORTH SPENDING YOUR TIME AND LIFE ON?

WHEN YOU ARE ON YOUR DEATHBED, DO YOU EXPECT YOU'LL BE PROUD OF WHAT YOU'VE ACCOMPLISHED IN YOUR LIFE?

IF YOU WERE TO DIE TOMORROW, WOULD YOU BE SATISFIED WITH WHAT YOU'VE ACCOMPLISHED SO FAR?

IF SO, IS YOUR LIFE COMPLETE?

WHAT MORE WOULD YOU LIKE TO DO IN YOUR LIFETIME?

IF NOT, WHY NOT?

WILL THE WORK YOU LEAVE BEHIND BE OF INTEREST TO YOUR GRANDCHILDREN, OR TO FUTURE DESIGNERS?

IS YOUR WORK A JOB, A CAREER, OR A LIFE'S CALLING?

DO YOU LOOK FORWARD TO RETIREMENT?

IS WORKING A CHORE, OR A JOY?

WHAT'S YOUR DEFINITION

IF YOUR LIFE WERE A MOVIE, HOW WOULD YOU WRITE THE FINAL SCENE?

WOULD YOU LIKE ALL LOOSE ENDS TO BE TIED UP?

WHAT QUESTION WOULD YOU LIKE TO HAVE ANSWERED?

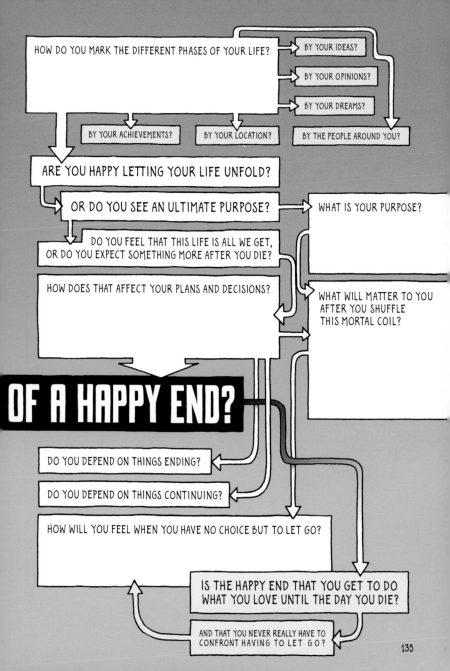

HOW DO YOU MARK THE DIFFERENT PHASES OF YOUR LIFE?

BY YOUR IDEAS?

BY YOUR OPINIONS?

BY YOUR DREAMS?

BY YOUR ACHIEVEMENTS?

BY YOUR LOCATION?

BY THE PEOPLE AROUND YOU?

ARE YOU HAPPY LETTING YOUR LIFE UNFOLD?

OR DO YOU SEE AN ULTIMATE PURPOSE?

WHAT IS YOUR PURPOSE?

DO YOU FEEL THAT THIS LIFE IS ALL WE GET,
OR DO YOU EXPECT SOMETHING MORE AFTER YOU DIE?

HOW DOES THAT AFFECT YOUR PLANS AND DECISIONS?

WHAT WILL MATTER TO YOU
AFTER YOU SHUFFLE
THIS MORTAL COIL?

OF A HAPPY END?

DO YOU DEPEND ON THINGS ENDING?

DO YOU DEPEND ON THINGS CONTINUING?

HOW WILL YOU FEEL WHEN YOU HAVE NO CHOICE BUT TO LET GO?

IS THE HAPPY END THAT YOU GET TO DO
WHAT YOU LOVE UNTIL THE DAY YOU DIE?

AND THAT YOU NEVER REALLY HAVE TO
CONFRONT HAVING TO LET GO?

WHAT WOULD LETTERING TEACHER AND LOGOTYPE DESIGNER

DOYALD YOUNG

LIKE TO KNOW?

WHAT ARE YOUR STRONG POINTS?

WHAT ARE YOUR WEAK ONES?

HOW DO YOU PLAN TO IMPROVE THE WEAK ONES?

ARE YOU IMPROVING YOUR VOCABULARY DAILY?

ARE YOU SURE THAT YOU'VE SELECTED THE RIGHT MAJOR?

HOW WILL YOU IMPROVE YOUR PRESENTATION SKILLS?

HAVE YOU LEARNED TO WRITE A GOOD BUSINESS LETTER?

DO YOU PLAN TO STUDY ABROAD?

GEORGE WILL IN A COMMENCEMENT ADDRESS ADVISED AGAINST MARRIAGE BEFORE AGE 21, AND CHILDREN BEFORE 25 TO EASE THE BURDEN OF EDUCATION.

HAVE YOU SAVED SOME MONEY?

HAVE YOU FOUND OUT WHO YOU ARE?

HAVE YOU RESET YOUR GOALS?

HAVE YOU MET YOUR ORIGINAL GOALS?

IS THIS THE TIME TO RAISE A FAMILY?

HAVE YOU TRIED TO BUY A HOUSE?

SHOULD YOU HAVE TAKEN A REFRESHER COURSE?

HOW MUCH PR HAVE YOU DONE FOR YOURSELF?

DO YOU STILL FIND DESIGN SATISFYING?

IF NOT, HAVE YOU THOUGHT OF THE BLISS THAT JOSEPH CAMPBELL SPEAKS OF?

HAVE YOU MADE A WILL? IT'S NOT TOO SOON.

ARE YOUR INVESTMENTS SECURE?

ARE YOU HAPPY, AND IF NOT, WHY?

IS YOUR LOVED ONE HAPPY?

HAVE YOU DONE SOME CHARITY WORK?

WOODROW WILSON SAID THAT WE ARE PUT HERE TO IMPROVE THE WORLD. *HAVE YOU REMEMBERED THE TASK?*

HAVE YOU REMEMBERED TO BE KIND?

HAVE YOU REALIZED YOUR YOUTHFUL DREAMS?

WHAT ARE YOUR FUTURE PLANS?

HAVE YOU MADE A LIST OF THE TEN MOST IMPORTANT THINGS IN YOUR LIFE?

WHAT'S NUMBER ONE?

WHAT'S ON YOUR SMALL LIST?

WHAT DO YOU WANT TO DO?

WHAT'S ON YOUR BIG LIST?

WHAT'S THE FIRST THING YOU'LL DO

WHO WILL YOU TALK TO?

WHEN YOU CLOSE THIS BOOK?

WHAT WILL YOU MAKE?

53 **Sean Adams** is a co-founder of AdamsMorioka. He is the co-author of *Logo Design Workbook, Color Design Workbook,* and *Masters of Design.* He is a national President ex officio of AIGA, a Fellow of the Aspen Design Conference, and teaches at Art Center College of Design. → adamsmorioka.com

86 **Jed Alger** is a writer. After 20 years as a copywriter and creative director at Hill Holiday, Ogilvy & Mather, and Wieden + Kennedy he now focuses on writing, concepting, and strategy under the *Jed Co.* banner. → jedalger.com

17 **Judd Apatow** is the writer/director of *The 40-Year-Old Virgin, Knocked Up,* and *Funny People,* and has produced more than two dozen movies, including *Anchorman* and *Superbad.* He was an executive producer for *The Larry Sanders Show, The Ben Stiller Show, Freaks & Geeks,* and *Undeclared,* which he also created. → @juddapatow

134 **Marian Bantjes** is a designer, typographer, writer, and illustrator working internationally from her base on a small island off the west coast of Canada. She is known for her detailed and lovingly precise vector art, her obsessive hand work, her patterning and ornament. She is the author of the book *i wonder.* → bantjes.com

128 **Ken Carbone** is a designer, artist, musician, author, and teacher. He is the co-founder and chief creative director of the Carbone Smolan Agency, a design and branding company in New York City. He is the author of *The Virtuoso: Face to Face with 40 Extraordinary Talents.* He blogs about design for *Fast Company.* → carbonesmolan.com

116 **Tim Carvell** is the head writer for *The Daily Show with Jon Stewart.* He also writes the "Planet Tad" column for *Mad Magazine,* and has written for *Fortune Magazine, McSweeney's Quarterly Concern, The New York Times, Modern Humorist, Entertainment Weekly,* and *Slate.com.* → @timcarvell

78 **Deanne Cheuk** is an artist and designer. She has been commissioned by American Express, Dell, Levi's, Nike, Target, MTV, The Gap, Urban Outfitters, Juicy Couture, *The Guardian,* and *The New York Times Magazine* for her illustrative type, illustration, and art direction. Her first book is called *Mushroom Girls Virus.* → deannecheuk.com

91 **Doug Chiang** is an Academy Award®-winning film designer and artist. He worked on films such as *Terminator 2: Judgment Day* and *Forrest Gump,* and served as design director for Lucasfilm on *Star Wars Episode I* and *Star Wars Episode II.* He was a production designer on *The Polar Express* and *Beowulf,* and collaborated with author Orson Scott Card on the illustrated sci-fi book *Robota.* → dchiang.com

51 **Wayne Coyne** is the multiple Grammy® Award-winning lead singer, lyricist, and principal songwriter for the band The Flaming Lips. He is a painter, and experimental artist, and filmmaker. In 2009, his song, "Do You Realize??" was declared the official rock song of the State of Oklahoma by executive order. → flaminglips.com

47 **Russell M. Davies** is an author, strategist, and advertising person. He is a head of planning at Ogilvy, a partner at RIG, and a founder of Newspaper Club. He writes a column for *Campaign* and another for *Wired,* as well as the blogs *a good place for a cup of tea and a think* and *eggbaconchipsandbeans,* which became a book. → russelldavies.com

63 **Tarsem Singh Dhandwar** is the director of the *The Cell, The Fall,* and *Immortals.* His commercials and music videos have won countless awards, including the Cannes Grand Prix Award, eight MTV Awards, and a Grammy®, and are part of the permanent collection of the Museum of Modern Art in New York. → tarsem.org

126 **Arem Duplessis** is the design director of *The New York Times Magazine.* He has held design-director and art-director positions at titles including *Spin, GQ,* and *Blaze* magazines. *The New York Times Magazine* was most recently awarded 'Design Team of the Year' by The Art Directors Club. → nytimes.com/pages/magazine

103 **Dave Eggers** is the author of seven books, including *What Is the What,* and *Zeitoun.* He is the founder and editor of *McSweeney's,* and co-founder of 826 National, a network of nonprofit writing and tutoring centers for youth. → mcsweeneys.net

95 **Karen Fowler** is the Emmy Award®-winning executive producer of *The Electric Company* and the creative director of its offshoot, *Prankster Planet,* a 360° interactive learning/gaming experience for kids. She spent five years at Nickelodeon's Creative Lab before making other breakthrough series for Sesame Workshop. She likes → funnychangemakers.com

22 **Jona Frank** is a photographer and director. Her books include *High School* and *Right: Portraits from the Evangelical Ivy League.* Her work has been exhibited internationally and is in several prominent collections, including the J. Paul Getty Museum and SFMOMA. She is at work on a series of photos about a group of boys in Southern California. → jonafrank.com

31 **Ze Frank** is a digital age storyteller. He rose to Internet fame in 2001 with his viral video *How To Dance Properly* and has been making online art toys and collaborative play spaces ever since. His groundbreaking videoblog *The Show With Ze Frank* is now celebrating its fifth anniversary. Ze is now the president of making people feel awesome at star.me → zefrank.com

76 **Jill Greenberg** is an award-winning and often controversial photographer who straddles the line between assignments and her own personal work. Her books include *Bear Portraits, Monkey Portraits,* and catalogs for her shows *Ursine* and *End Times.* Her clients include Universal Pictures, HBO, *New York Magazine,* and Microsoft. → manipulator.com

52 **Stanley Hainsworth** is the founder of Tether. Previously, Hainsworth was VP of global creative for Starbucks. He also spent 12 years at Nike as a creative director and another four as global creative director at Lego. He has used his various hairstyles to great effect in various and sundry homeless and 'bad guy' roles in movies, stage, and television. → tetherinc.com

124 **Peter Hannan** is the creator and executive producer of the Nickelodeon animated television series *CatDog.* He also wrote and sang the *CatDog* theme song. He is the author and illustrator of *The Sillyville Saga,* the *Super Goofballs* series, and another series of young adult illustrated novels called *Wally, King of Flurb.* → peterhannan.com

101 **Debbie Millman** is president of the design division at Sterling Brands, host of the radio show *Design Matters,* and a design blogger for *Fast Company.* She is the author of the books *How To Think Like A Great Graphic Designer, Essential Principles of Graphic Design, Look Both Ways,* and *Brand Thinking and Other Noble Pursuits.* → debbiemillman.com

67 **Rick Morris** is a classically trained, self-taught artist/illustrator who successfully transitioned into the world of motion graphics. His works have appeared as opening titles for films such as *Mi Vida Loca* and *The Big Tease,* on TV programs such as *The Sopranos,* and in commercials for Toyota, Panasonic, and Nike. → **nobleassassins.com** + **rockhoneystudio.com**

114 **Seth Morris** (aka Bob Ducca) is a writer and actor. He currently writes for *Funny Or Die* and sometimes acts in different TV shows and movies. → **funnyordie.com/seth**

119 **Christoph Niemann** is an illustrator whose work has appeared on the covers of *The New Yorker, Newsweek, Wired,* and *The New York Times Magazine.* He is the author of many books, among them *The Pet Dragon, I LEGO N.Y.* and *SUBWAY,* based on *The Boys and the Subway,* the first entry of his *Abstract City* blog. → **christophniemann.com**

83 **David Norland** is a composer for film and television. His work includes the acclaimed score for the documentary *Anvil! The Story of Anvil,* and commercials for Acura, Lexus, and Range Rover. After rising to prominence as half of the electronica duo Solar Twins, he now produces artists such as Frankmusik and UK soprano Helen White. → **davidnorland.com**

122 **Patton Oswalt** is an American stand-up comedian, writer, and actor. His comedy albums include *Feelin' Kinda Patton, Werewolves and Lollipops,* and the Grammy®-nominated *My Weakness Is Strong.* He is the author of the book *Zombie Spaceship Wasteland,* and starred in numerous films including *Big Fan* and *Ratatouille.* → **pattonoswalt.com**

81 **Martha Rich** is an acclaimed illustrator and teacher. She obsessively paints underwear, wigs, lobsters, and Loretta Lynn. She is currently back in Philadelphia studying for her MFA in Painting at the University of Pennsylvania. → **martharich.com**

106 **Stefan Sagmeister** is a two-time Grammy® Award-winning graphic designer. He has designed albums for Lou Reed, OK Go, The Rolling Stones, and David Byrne. His work has been profiled in *The New York Times* and *Rolling Stone.* He is the author of the books *Made You Look* and *Things I Have Learned In My Life So Far.* → **sagmeister.com**

39 **Meredith Scardino** parlayed degrees in painting from Cornell and Parsons into a job for animation maverick Bill Plympton, writing for VH-1's *Best Week Ever, The Late Show with David Letterman,* and winning two Emmy® Awards for her work as a writer on *The Colbert Report.* → **wn.com/Meredith_Scardino**

121 **J.J. Sedelmaier** is an animation director, designer, and producer of commercials and animated shorts. With Robert Smigel he created *The Ambiguously Gay Duo, The X-Presidents,* and *Fun With Real Audio* for SNL. His company, J.J. Sedelmaier Productions, Inc. launched the first season of MTV's "Beavis and Butthead" series in 1993. → **jjsedelmaier.com**

43 **Dave Stewart** is a prodigious musician, producer, and entrepreneur. Co-founder of Eurythmics, he has also written with and produced an array of legendary artists. Dave co-wrote the book *The Business Playground: Where Creativity and Commerce Collide.* → **davestewart.com**

132 **Lara Tomlin** is an illustrator specializing in hand-tinted copper-plate etchings. Her work appears in the pages of *The New Yorker, The New York Times, Forbes, Time Magazine, Manhattan Theater Club, The Financial Times, Harvard Business Review, Garden & Gun Magazine,* and the *Bulletin of Atomic Scientists.* → **theispot.com/artist/tomlin**

75 **Jakob Trollbäck** is a self-taught designer from Sweden. He leads Trollbäck + Company, an innovative and highly successful company, creates seminal and award-winning designs, and is an acknowledged industry leader in branding and immersive motion graphic design. He has presented at the TED Conference. He is a DJ. → **trollback.com**

85 **Rick Valicenti,** founder and principal of Thirst (3st.com), has been creating and designing for 30 years. His work has been featured in every major graphic design publication, and in person with designers and students on six continents. Rick is editor and author of the book *Emotion As Promotion – The Book of Thirst,* published by Monacelli Press. → **3st.com**

18 **Armin Vit** is the co-founder, with his wife Bryony Gomez-Palacio, of UnderConsideration, a graphic design firm and publishing enterprise all rolled into one. Together they have authored a number of books on graphic design, the most recent efforts being *Graphic Design, Referenced* and the self-published *Flaunt.* → **underconsideration.com**

111 **Esther Pearl Watson** is an illustrator and comic book artist. She is the author of the comic *Unlovable* and—with her husband Mark Todd—of the book *Whatcha Mean, What's A 'Zine?—The Art of Making Zines and Mini-Comics.* → **estherwatson.com**

113 **Lynda Weinman** is best known as the author of numerous web design books, the co-founder, with her husband Bruce Heavin, of lynda.com, and the co-founder of the Flashforward Conference & Film Festival. She rotoscoped the empirial throne room scene on the Death Star in *Star Wars Episode VI: Return of the Jedi.* → **lynda.com**

99 **Jan Wilker** is the co-founder of karlssonwilker inc., the internationally renowned New York design agency. Wilker and co-founder Hjalti Karlsson published a book about their studio, *tellmewhy—The First 24 Months of a New York Design Company,* which offers an honest portrayal of setting up a design studio as well as raising a smile. → **karlssonwilker.com**

136 **Doyald Young** was a teacher and designer specializing in logotypes, corporate alphabets, and typefaces. His creations include Young Baroque, ITC Éclat, Home Run, and the formal script Young Gallant. He wrote and designed the books *Logotypes & Letterforms, Fonts & Logos, Dangerous Curves,* and the forthcoming *Learning Curves.* → **doyaldyoung.com**

Stefan G. Bucher is the author and designer of the books *All Access—The Making of Thirty Extraordinary Graphic Designers, 100 Days of Monsters, The Graphic Eye,* and *You Deserve A Medal.* He has created designs for Sting, David Hockney, and *The New York Times.* His time-lapse drawings appear on the TV show *The Electric Company* on PBS and on his Daily Monster® blog. → **344design.com + dailymonster.com**

IN LOVING MEMORY of my kind friends and wonderful teachers, Norm Schureman and Doyald Young.

THANK YOU to Nikki Echler McDonald, Tracey Croom, and Glenn Bisignani at Peachpit, Joel Arquillos, Hank Bedford, Stephen Berkman, Tom Biederbeck, Allison Bond, Alyson Buoncristiani, Meagan Day, Bill Eckenrod, Kristin Ellison, Christopher Farah, Liz Farrelly, Lenny Feldsott, Karla Field, Jeff Fischer, Christina Galante, Rick Gershon, Bruce Heavin, Jim Heimann, Natalia Ilyin, Lisa Jann, Matthew Knott-Craig, Sharon Ludtke, David Mayes, Tim Moraitis, Pat McGuire, Jennifer Morita, Marcia Mosko, Steven Moss, Emily Potts, Peter S. Sloane, Jennifer Stone, Terry Stone, Mark Sylvester, Amanda Van Goethen, Suzanne Wertheim, Emily Wong, Simon Zirkunow, and *Vielen Dank* to my Mom & Dad, of course. Special thanks to my kind, patient, and generally wonderful girlfriend Andy Mallett.

WATCH
READ
CREATE

Unlimited online access to all Peachpit, Adobe
Press, Apple Training and New Riders videos
and books, as well as content from other
leading publishers including: O'Reilly Media,
Focal Press, Sams, Que, Total Training, John
Wiley & Sons, Course Technology PTR, Class
on Demand, VTC and more.

No time commitment or contract required!
Sign up for one month or a year.
All for $19.99 a month

SIGN UP TODAY
peachpit.com/creativeedge